The Ultimate Diabetes Cookbook

Quick & Easy Friendly Recipes To Prevent, Control And Live Well With Diabetes.

Betty Ryan

© **Copyright 2021**

The content contained within this book may not be reproduced, duplicated or transmitted without direct written permission from the author or the publisher.

Under no circumstances will any blame or legal responsibility be held against the publisher, or author, for any damages, reparation, or monetary loss due to the information contained within this book. Either directly or indirectly.

Legal Notice:

This book is copyright protected. This book is only for personal use. You cannot amend, distribute, sell, use, quote or paraphrase any part, or the content within this book, without the consent of the author or publisher.

Disclaimer Notice:

Please note the information contained within this document is for educational and entertainment purposes only. All effort has been executed to present accurate, up to date, and reliable, complete information. No warranties of any kind are declared or implied. Readers acknowledge that the author is not engaging in the rendering of legal, financial, medical or professional advice. The content within this book has been derived from various sources. Please consult a licensed professional before attempting any techniques outlined in this book.

By reading this document, the reader agrees that under no circumstances is the author responsible for any losses, direct or indirect, which are incurred as a result of the use of information contained within this document, including, but not limited to, — errors, omissions, or inaccuracies.

Introduction 8

What is Diabetes? 11

Gestational Diabetes Causes 19

Foods to Eat 26

Foods to Avoid 32

Breakfast 37

    Berry-Oat Breakfast Bars 37

    Whole-Grain Breakfast Cookies 40

    Blueberry Breakfast Cake 42

    Buckwheat Grouts Breakfast Bowl 47

    Peach Muesli Bake 49

    Steel-Cut Oatmeal Bowl 51

    with Fruit and Nuts 51

    Whole-Grain Dutch Baby Pancake 53

    Mushroom, Zucchini and Onion Frittata 55

    Spinach and Cheese Quiche 57

    Spicy Jalapeno Popper Deviled Eggs 59

    Lovely Porridge 60

    Salty Macadamia Chocolate Smoothie 62

    Cinnamon and Coconut Porridge 64

    An Omelet of Swiss Chard 66

    Cheesy Low-Carb Omelet 67

    Bacon and Chicken Garlic Wrap 69

Grilled Chicken Platter...71

Parsley Chicken Breast...72

Mustard Chicken..74

Balsamic Chicken..75

Greek Chicken Breast..78

Chipotle Lettuce Chicken...79

Lunch 82

Grilled Tempeh with Pineapple..82

Courgettes in Cider Sauce 85

Baked Mixed Mushrooms..87

Spiced Okra 90

Lemony Salmon Burgers 93

Caprese Turkey Burgers..94

Pasta Salad..96

Chicken, Strawberry and Avocado Salad 98

Spinach Salad with Bacon...101

Cauliflower Rice with Chicken...102

Turkey with Fried Eggs..104

Kale and White Bean Stew 105

Slow Cooker Two-Bean Sloppy Joes.................................108

Lighter Eggplant Parmesan...110

Coconut-Lentil Curry 113

Stuffed Portobello with Cheese...115

Lighter Shrimp Scampi 118

Maple-Mustard Salmon...120

Chicken Salad with Grapes and Pecans 122

- Roasted Vegetables 125
- Millet Pilaf 128
- Sweet and Sour Onions 130
- Sautéed Apples and Onions 131
- Zucchini Noodles with 133
- Portobello Mushrooms 133

Dinner 136
- Cauliflower Mac and Cheese 136
- Easy Egg Salad 138
- Baked Chicken Legs 140
- Creamed Spinach 141
- Stuffed Mushrooms 143
- Vegetable Soup 144
- Pork Chop Diane 146
- Autumn Pork Chops with 148
- Red Cabbage and Apples 148
- Chipotle Chili Pork Chops 150
- Orange-Marinated Pork Tenderloin 152
- Homestyle Herb Meatballs 154
- Lime-Parsley Lamb Cutlets 155
- Mediterranean Steak Sandwiches 157
- Roasted Beef with 159
- Peppercorn Sauce 159
- Coffee-and-Herb-Marinated Steak 161
- Traditional Beef Stroganoff 163
- Chicken and Roasted Vegetable Wraps 165

Spicy Chicken Cacciatore 167

Scallion Sandwich 169

Lean Lamb and Turkey Meatballs with Yogurt 171

Air Fried Section and Tomato 173

Cheesy Salmon Fillets 175

Salmon with Asparagus 177

Shrimp in Garlic Butter 179

Cobb Salad 181

Salad 183

Thai Quinoa Salad 183

Green Goddess Bowl and 185

Avocado Cumin Dressing 185

Sweet and Savory Salad 187

Kale Pesto's Pasta 189

Beet Salad with Basil Dressing 190

Basic Salad with Olive Oil Dressing 192

Spinach and Orange Salad with Oil Drizzle 194

Fruit Salad with Coconut-Lime Dressing 195

Cranberry and Brussels Sprouts with Dressing 197

Parsnip, Carrot, and Kale Salad with Dressing 199

Tomato Toasts 200

Every Day Salad 202

Super-Seedy Salad with Tahini Dressing 203

Vegetable Salad 205

Greek Salad 206

Alkaline Spring Salad 208

Fresh Tuna Salad 209
Roasted Portobello Salad 211
Shredded Chicken Salad 213
Broccoli Salad 214
Cherry Tomato Salad 216
Ground Turkey Salad 218
Asian Cucumber Salad 220
Cauliflower Tofu Salad 221
Scallop Caesar Salad 224

Introduction

Diabetes is a disease in which blood glucose, also called blood sugar, doesn't get properly regulated. Glucose is the form of sugar that's used by all cells for energy. In diabetes, the body either doesn't produce enough insulin or can't use the insulin that's produced. This a type of disease that occurs when the pancreas can't produce enough insulin, a hormone that is used to help cells use glucose (sugar) for energy. Diabetics must monitor their glucose levels regularly and take insulin to make sure the glucose stays within the normal range.

Diabetes symptoms include excessive thirst, frequent urination, hunger, blurred vision, unexplained weight loss, and sudden numbness or weakness of the arms or legs. Diabetics also experienced excessive sweating, itching, and a dry mouth.

Diabetes is also a disease associated with blood sugar i.e., the concentration of sugar in the blood that the body is unable to maintain within normal limits. Hyperglycemia occurs when blood glucose exceeds 100 mg./dl fastings or 140 mg/dl two hours after a meal. This condition may depend on a defect in function or a deficit in the production of insulin, the hormone secreted by the pancreas, used for the metabolism of sugars and other components of food to be transformed into energy for the whole organism (such as petrol for the engine).

When blood glucose levels are twice equal to or greater than 126 mg./dl, diabetes is diagnosed. High blood glucose levels—if not treated—over time, lead to chronic complications with damage to the kidneys, retina, nerves peripheral, and cardiovascular system (heart and arteries).

If you do have diabetes, the body either does not produce enough insulin or utilizes it as effectively as it should. A large amount of blood sugar stays in your system when there is insufficient insulin or when cells don't react to insulin. It can lead to major health issues like heart disease, eyesight loss, and renal illness over time.

Although there is no treatment for diabetes, decreasing weight, eating healthy foods, and being active can all help. Taking medication as needed, receiving diabetes self-management assistance and training, and keeping health-care appointments can help lessen the impact diabetes has on your life.

Insulin is required for our survival. It serves an important purpose. It enables blood glucose to reach our cells and provides energy to our bodies. Your body continuously breaks down carbohydrates from food and drinks and converts them to glucose if you have type 2 diabetes. The pancreas subsequently releases insulin in response to this. However, since this insulin is unable to function correctly, your blood glucose levels continue to rise. More insulin is produced as a result of this.

To prevent or manage diabetes, eat a tasty, well-balanced food intake that will keep your energy boosted and help you feel better about your lifestyle.

What is Diabetes?

Diabetes mellitus is a set of illnesses impair your body's ability to utilize blood sugar (glucose). Because glucose is a key form of energy for the cells that form your muscles and tissues, it is essential to your health. It's also the main source of energy for your brain. The root reason for diabetes differs depending on the kind. However, regardless of the kind of diabetes people have, it may cause an excess of sugar in the blood.

Type 1 diabetes, as well as type 2 diabetes, are both chronic diabetic diseases. Prediabetes or gestational diabetes are two diabetes disorders that may be reversible. You have prediabetes when your blood glucose levels become higher than normal but not strong enough to be categorized as diabetes. And, unless proper steps are taken to avoid development, prediabetes is frequently the prelude to diabetes. Gestational diabetes develops throughout pregnancy, although it may go away after the baby is born.

Diabetes develops when your body's cells cannot absorb sugar (glucose) and utilize it for energy. Extra sugar builds up in your system because of this. Diabetes that is not well controlled can have catastrophic effects, including damage to various organs and tissues in your body, including one's heart, kidneys, eyes, and nerves.

Breaking down the food you eat to multiple nutrient sources is part of the digestion process. Your body turns carbs (such as bread, rice, or pasta) into sugar whenever you consume them (glucose). When glucose enters your circulation, it needs help – a "key" – to get to its final destination: our body's tissues (cells create your tissues and organs). Insulin is the "helper" or "key."

1.1: Types of Diabetes

1. **Type 1 Diabetes:** In this illness, your body fights against itself. Your pancreas' insulin-producing cells are damaged in this situation. Type 1 diabetes affects approximately 10% of those with diabetes. It's most often seen in kids and young people, although it may strike anybody at any age. Diabetes was previously referred to as "juvenile." Insulin is required for Type 1 diabetics daily. Insulin-dependent diabetes is the name given to it because of this.

2. **Type 2 Diabetes:** This kind occurs when your body does not produce enough insulin. Type 2 diabetes affects approximately 95% of diabetes, typical individuals in their forties and fifties. Type 2 diabetes is also known as adult-onset diabetes or insulin-resistant diabetes. It was probably referred to as "having a bit of sugar" by your parents or grandparents.

3. **Prediabetes:** This is the period before the onset of Type 2 diabetes. The blood sugar levels are higher than usual but not strong enough for Type 2 diabetes to be diagnosed.

4. **Gestational Diabetes:** Some women acquire this kind throughout their pregnancy. Gestational diabetes typically disappears following the birth of a child. If you do have gestational diabetes, though, you're more likely to acquire Type 2 diabetes later in life.

1.2: Symptom of Diabetes

Depending on just how high your blood glucose is, the severity of diabetic symptoms varies. For some individuals, particularly those who have prediabetes, it's possible that they won't experience any symptoms at all.

Type 1 diabetes symptoms develop earlier and are more severe.

General Symptoms

The following are some most common diabetic symptoms:

- An increase in hunger
- An increase in thirst
- Weight reduction
- Urinating frequently
- Hazy vision
- Severe drowsiness
- Non-healing sores

Symptoms in women

Urinary tract infections, fungal infections, or dry, itchy skin are all signs of diabetes in women.

Symptoms in men

Men with diabetes may have erectile dysfunction (ED), or low muscular strength, in addition to the typical symptoms of diabetes.

Symptoms of Type 1 Diabetes

The following are some of the signs or symptoms for type 1 diabetes:

- Severe hunger
- Thirst has increased
- Unintended weight loss
- Urination becomes frequent.
- Eyesight problems
- Tiredness
- It may also cause mood swings.

Symptoms of Type 2 Diabetes

Type 2 diabetes symptoms include:

- An increase in hunger
- An increase in thirst
- Urination has risen
- Hazy vision
- Tiredness

- Slow-healing sores

It's also possible that it'll lead to recurrent infections. It is because high levels of glucose make it hard for the person to recover.

1.3: Causes of Diabetes

To comprehend diabetes, you must first comprehend how glucose is typically metabolized in the human body.

Insulin's mechanism of action

- It is released into the circulation by the pancreas.
- It circulates throughout your body, allowing glucose to
- enter the cells.
- It is a hormone that reduces the quantity of sugar in the blood.

The quantity of insulin your pancreas secretes decreases as your blood sugar lowers.

Glucose's Function

The cells that form muscles and other tissues use glucose, some sugar, as an energy source.

- Food and the liver are the two main sources of glucose.

- Sugar is taken into the circulation and, with the assistance of insulin, penetrates cells.

- The liver both stores and produces glucose.

- When your sugar levels have dropped, including when you have still not eaten in a while, your body breaks down glycogen into glucose that maintains a normal glucose level.

Type 1 Diabetes causes

Type 1 diabetes has an unknown etiology. What is known would be that your immune system, which is usually responsible for fighting dangerous germs and viruses, targets and kills your pancreas' insulin-producing cells. Glucose piles up in your circulation instead of being delivered to your cells. You will have very little or even no insulin because of this.

Type 1 diabetes is believed to be caused by a mix of genetic predisposition and environmental factors, but the precise nature of those variables is unknown. Weight isn't thought to have a role in type 1 diabetes.

Prediabetes and Type 2 Diabetes causes

The cells grow resistant to the effects of insulin in prediabetes — which may progress to type 2 diabetes — and type 2 diabetes, and your pancreas is unable to produce enough insulin that overcomes this resistance. Sugar accumulates up in your circulation instead of going into your cells, where it is required for energy.

It's unclear why this occurs, but genetic and environmental variables glucose pile up in your circulation instead of being delivered to your cells. are thought to have a role throughout the development of diabetes. Although being overweight is closely related to the development of diabetes, not everyone who has the disease is obese.

Gestational Diabetes Causes

Insulin resistance is increased in your cells because of these chemicals.

Your pancreas normally reacts by generating enough additional insulin to address this resistance. However, your pancreas can't always keep up. When this occurs, too little glucose enters your cells while too much remains in your blood, causing gestational diabetes.

1.4: Prevention and Treatment

It is almost impossible to avoid Type 1 diabetes. However, the very same making lifestyle changes that aid in the treatment of prediabetes, type 2 diabetes, and gestational diabetes may also aid in their prevention:

1. **Consume nutritious foods:** Reduce the amount of fat and calories you consume while increasing your fiber intake, avoid boredom, strive for diversity.

2. **Increase your physical activity:** Aim for a minimum of 150 minutes of medium aerobic exercise each week, or approximately 30 minutes of aerobic activity physical activity daily of the week.

3. **Get rid of the extra pounds:** If you're overweight, even the slightest weight change may lower your diabetes risk. However, don't attempt to reduce weight when pregnant. Focus on long-term adjustments to your diet and activity habits to maintain a healthy weight. Remember the advantages of reducing weight, such as a healthier heart, greater energy, and better self-esteem, to keep yourself motivated.

Metformin and other oral diabetic medications may lower the risk of type 2 diabetes, but good lifestyle choices are still necessary. Make sure you have your sugar levels tested at most once a year to ensure you don't have type 2 diabetes.

Diabetes treatment is determined by the kind of diabetes you have, how well your blood sugar is managed, and any other medical problems you may have. If you have Type 2 diabetes, you may need medicines (for both diabetes and illnesses that seem to be risk factors for type 2), insulin, and lifestyle modifications such as reducing weight, eating healthier, and exercising more.

1.5: Link with Obesity

While the specific main risk factors are unknown, it is known that several variables increase the chance of having various forms of diabetes mellitus. Being obese or overweight with a body mass index (BMI) of 30 or above is a risk factor for type 2 diabetes.

Obesity is thought to be responsible for 80-85% of the risk of getting type 2 diabetes. A new study indicates that obese individuals are up to 80 considerably more probable than someone with a BMI of less than 22 to acquire type 2 diabetes.

It is common knowledge that being overweight or obese increases your chance of getting type 2 diabetes, especially if you carry extra weight around your belly.

According to studies, abdominal obesity causes fat cells to generate 'proinflammatory' substances, making the body less responsive to the insulin produced by altering insulin-responsive cells' activity and capacity to react to insulin.

Insulin resistance is a defining feature underlying type 2 diabetes. Central or abdomen obesity is a high-risk type of obesity defined by excess fat tissue (i.e., a big waistline).

Obesity is also believed to cause metabolic alterations in the body. Fat tissue releases fat compounds into the bloodstream due to these alterations, impacting insulin-responsive cells and decreasing insulin sensitivity.

Obesity promotes prediabetes, a metabolic state that nearly invariably progresses to type 2 diabetes.

1.6: Controlling sugar levels with Diet

You don't need any special meals if you're attempting to avoid or manage diabetes since your nutritional requirements are essentially the same as anyone else's. However, you must pay attention to certain of your dietary choices, particularly the carbs you consume. While adopting the

Mediterranean or even another heart-healthy diet may assist, losing a little weight is an essential thing you can do.

You may decrease your sugar levels, blood pressure, or cholesterol levels by losing only 5% to 10% of your overall weight. Losing weight while eating a better diet may improve your attitude, energy, and overall well-being. Patients with diabetes have a nearly doubled risk of heart attack and are more prone to acquire mental health problems like depression.

In most cases, however, type 2 diabetes may be prevented, and in some cases, it can even be reversed. By eating healthier, becoming more active and healthier, and losing weight, you may be able to reduce your symptoms.

1.7: Advice and Guidelines

You're aware that controlling type 2 diabetes entails more than simply taking medication. So, you've been striving to eat healthier and live a healthier lifestyle. However, determining what is and is not healthy may be difficult.

Consider the following habits. They may seem to be beneficial, yet they may be working against you.

1. Purchasing goods that are "sugar-free"

Many items at the store seem to be diabetes-friendly since they do not include added sugar. However, many sugar alternatives include carbohydrates. That implies they have the potential to raise your blood sugar levels.

Check the nutrition information before adding anything to your basket to discover how many grams of carbohydrates are in each portion or how much sweetener is added. Knowing how many carbohydrates are in each serving of food may help you keep track of your blood glucose levels.

2. Substituting meal replacement bars for regular meals

Weight loss may assist, and nutritional supplement bars may seem a simple method to lose weight.

Athletes are the target market for several meal replacement products. As a result, they may be rich in calories. Others include sugar alcohols in them, which may cause gastrointestinal issues.

When you're short on time, it's OK to have a bar for the morning if you pay close attention to the nutrition information. However, actual meals or calorie restricted snacks that are full meals and nutritionally complete are preferable.

3. Supplementing with vitamins and minerals

A diet rich in vegetables should provide all the nutrients people need. While a multivitamin will help fill the gaps, nothing beats the real thing: food.

Some individuals use cinnamon or chromium supplements to attempt to keep their blood sugar levels under control. These may or not be beneficial. If you decide to take these — or any supplement — talk to your doctor first. They can ensure that it is safe for you and will not interfere with any medications.

4. Keeping away from any high-fat meals

If you eat the proper types of fat, just little fat is healthy for you. Saturated fats found in meat and milk should be limited, and trans fats should be avoided entirely.

Nuts eaten with higher-carb meals may help to maintain blood sugar levels from rising too quickly. Avocado eaters are much less likely to develop metabolic syndrome, according to another research. It is a group of symptoms that involves elevated blood sugar levels.

5. Snack packets containing 100 calories

Since each seems to be so little, many individuals open pack after pack. They consume more than they would have if they had begun with a "normal" container. People who have been given nine tiny bags of chips ate almost twice as many as those given two big bags in one research.

Foods to Eat

Vegetables

Fresh vegetables never cause harm to anyone. So, adding a meal full of vegetables is the best shot for all diabetic patients. But not all vegetables contain the same number of macronutrients. Some vegetables contain a high amount of carbohydrates, so those are not suitable for a diabetic diet. We need to use vegetables which contain a low amount of carbohydrates.

1. Cauliflower
2. Spinach
3. Tomatoes
4. Broccoli
5. Lemons
6. Artichoke
7. Garlic
8. Asparagus
9. Spring onions
10. Onions
11. Ginger, etc.

Meat

Meat is not on the red list for the diabetic diet. It is fine to have some meat every now and then for diabetic patients. However certain meat types are better than others. For instance, red meat is not a preferable option for such patients. They should consume white meat more often whether it's seafood or poultry. Healthy options in meat are:

1. All fish
2. Scallops
3. Mussels
4. Shrimp
5. Oysters, etc.

Fruits

Not all fruits are good for diabetes. To know if the fruit is suitable for this diet, it is important to note its sugar content. Some fruits contain a high number of sugars in the form of sucrose and fructose, and those should be readily avoided. Here is the list of popularly used fruits that can be taken on the diabetic diet:

1. Peaches

2. Nectarines
3. Avocados
4. Apples
5. Berries
6. Grapefruit
7. Kiwi Fruit
8. Bananas
9. Cherries
10. Grapes
11. Orange
12. Pears
13. Plums
14. Strawberries

Nuts and Seeds

Nuts and seeds are perhaps the most enriched edibles, and they contain such a mix of macronutrients that can never harm anyone. So diabetic patients can take the nuts and seeds in their diet without any fear of a glucose spike.

1. Pistachios
2. Sunflower seeds
3. Walnuts

4. Peanuts
5. Pecans
6. Pumpkin seeds
7. Almonds
8. Sesame seeds, etc.

Grains

Diabetic patients should also be selective while choosing the right grains for their diet. The idea is to keep the amount of starch as minimum as possible. That is why you won't see any white rice in the list rather it is replaced with more fibrous brown rice.

1. Quinoa
2. Oats
3. Multigrain
4. Whole grains
5. Brown rice
6. Millet
7. Barley
8. Sorghum
9. Tapioca

Fats

Fat intake is the most debated topic as far as the diabetic diet is concerned. As there are diets like ketogenic, which are loaded with fats and still proved effective for diabetic patients. The key is the absence of carbohydrates. In any other situation, fats are as harmful to diabetics as any normal person. Switching to unsaturated fats is a better option.

1. Sesame oil
2. Olive oil
3. Canola oil
4. Grapeseed oil
5. Other vegetable oils
6. Fats extracted from plant sources

Diary

Any dairy product which directly or indirectly causes a glucose rise in the blood should not be taken on this diet. Other than those, all products are good to use. These items include:

1. Skimmed milk
2. Low-fat cheese
3. Eggs

4. Yogurt

5. Trans fat-free margarine or butter

Sugar Alternatives

Since ordinary sugars or sweeteners are strictly forbidden on a diabetic diet. There are artificial varieties that can add sweetness without raising the level of carbohydrates in the meal. These substitutes are:

1. Stevia

2. Xylitol

3. Natvia

4. Swerve

5. Monk fruit

6. Erythritol

Make sure to substitute them with extra care. The sweetness of each sweetener is entirely different from the table sugar, so add each in accordance with the intensity of their flavor. Stevia is the sweetest of them, and it should be used with more care. In place of 1 c of sugar, 1 tsp of stevia is enough. All other sweeteners are more or less similar to sugar in their intensity of sweetness.

Foods to Avoid

Knowing a general scheme of diet helps a lot, but it is equally important to be well familiar with the items which have to be avoided. With this list, you can make your diet 100 % sugar-free. There are many other food items that can cause some harm to a diabetic patient as the sugars do. So, let's discuss them in some detail here.

Sugars

Sugar is a big NO-GO for a diabetic diet. Once you are diabetic, you would need to say goodbye to all the natural sweeteners which are loaded with carbohydrates. They contain polysaccharides that readily break into glucose after getting into our body. And the list does not only include table sugars but other items like honey and molasses should also be avoided.

1. White sugar
2. Brown sugar
3. Confectionary sugar
4. Honey
5. Molasses
6. Granulated sugar

Your mind and your body, will not accept the abrupt change. It is recommended to go for a gradual change. It means start substituting it with low carb substitutes in a small amount, day by day.

High Fat Dairy Products

Once you are diabetic, you may get susceptible to a number of other fatal diseases including cardiovascular ones. That is why experts strictly recommend avoiding high-fat food products, especially dairy items. The high amount of fat can make your body insulin resistant. So even when you take insulin, it won't be of any use as the body will not work on it.

Saturated Animal Fats

Saturated animal fats are not good for anyone, whether diabetic or normal. So, better avoid using them in general. Whenever you are cooking meat, try to trim off all the excess fat. Cooking oils made out of these saturated fats should be avoided. Keep yourself away from any of the animal-origin fats.

High Carb Vegetables

As discussed above, vegetables with more starch are not suitable for diabetes. These veggies can increase the carbohydrate levels of food. So, omit these from the recipes and enjoy the rest of the less starchy vegetables. Some of the high carb vegetables are:

1. Potatoes
2. Sweet potatoes
3. Yams, etc.

Cholesterol Rich Ingredients

Bad cholesterol or high-density lipoprotein has the tendency to deposit in different parts of the body. That is why food items having high bad cholesterol are not good for diabetes. Such items should be replaced with the ones with low cholesterol.

High Sodium Products

Sodium is related to hypertension and blood pressure. Since diabetes is already the result of a hormonal imbalance in the body, in the presence of excess sodium—another imbalance—a fluid imbalance may occur which a diabetic body cannot tolerate. It adds up to already present complications of the disease. So, avoid using food items with a high amount of sodium. Mainly store packed items, processed foods, and salt all contain sodium, and one should avoid them all. Use only the unsalted variety of food products, whether it's butter, margarine, nuts, or other items.

Sugary Drinks

Cola drinks or other similar beverages are filled with sugars. If you had seen different video presentations showing the amount of the sugars present in a single bottle of soda, you would know how dangerous those are for diabetic patients. They can drastically increase the amount of blood glucose level within 30 minutes of drinking. Fortunately, there are many sugar-free varieties available in the drinks which are suitable for diabetic patients.

Sugar Syrups and Toppings

A number of syrups available in the markets are made out of nothing but sugar. Maple syrup is one good example. For a diabetic diet, the patient should avoid such sugary syrups and also stay away from the sugar-rich toppings available in the stores. If you want to use them at all, trust yourself and prepare them at home with a sugar-free recipe.

Sweet Chocolate and Candies

For diabetic patients, sugar-free chocolates or candies are the best way out. Other processed chocolate bars and candies are extremely damaging to their health, and all of these should be avoided. You can try and prepare healthy bars and candies at home with sugar-free recipes.

Alcohol

Alcohol has the tendency to reduce the rate of our metabolism and take away our appetite, which can render a diabetic patient into a very life-threatening condition. Alcohol in a very small amount cannot harm the patient, but the regular or constant intake of alcohol is bad for health and glucose levels.

Breakfast

Berry-Oat Breakfast Bars

Preparation time: 10 minutes

Cooking time: 25 minutes

Servings: 12

Ingredients:

- 2 c. fresh raspberries or blueberries
- 2 tbsps sugar
- 2 tbsps freshly squeezed lemon juice
- 1 tbsp. cornstarch
- 1 1/2 c. rolled oats
- 1/2 c. whole-wheat flour
- 1/2 c. walnuts
- 1/4 c. chia seeds
- 1/4 c. extra-virgin olive oil
- 1/4 c. honey
- 1 large egg

Directions:

1. Preheat the oven to 350 °F.
2. In a small saucepan over medium heat, stir together the berries, sugar, lemon juice, and cornstarch. Bring to a simmer. Reduce the heat and simmer for 2–3 minutes, until the mixture thickens.
3. In a food processor or high-speed blender, combine the oats, flour, walnuts, and chia seeds. Process until powdered. Add the olive oil, honey, and egg. Pulse a few more times, until well combined. Press half of the mixture into a 9-in. square baking dish.
4. Spread the berry filling over the oat mixture. Add the remaining oat mixture on top of the berries. Bake for 25 minutes, until browned.
5. Let cool completely, cut into 12 pieces, and serve. Store in a covered container for up to 5 days.

Nutrition:

Calories 201

Total fat 10 g.

Saturated fat 1 g.

Protein 5 g.

Carbohydrates 26 g.

Sugar 9 g.

Fiber 5 g.

Cholesterol 16 mg.

Sodium 8 mg.

Whole-Grain Breakfast Cookies

Preparation time: 20 minutes

Cooking time: 10 minutes

Servings: 18 cookies

Ingredients:

- 2 c. rolled oats
- 1/2 c. whole-wheat flour
- 1/4 c. ground flaxseed
- 1 tsp. baking powder
- 1 c. unsweetened applesauce
- 2 large eggs
- 2 tbsps vegetable oil
- 2 tsps. vanilla extract
- 1 tsp. ground cinnamon
- 1/2 c. dried cherries
- 1/4 c. unsweetened shredded coconut
- 2 oz. dark chocolate, chopped

Directions:

1. Preheat the oven to 350 °F.
2. In a large bowl, combine the oats, flour, flaxseed, and baking powder. Stir well to mix.
3. In a medium bowl, whisk the applesauce, eggs, vegetable oil, vanilla, and cinnamon. Pour the wet mixture into the dry mixture, and stir until combined.
4. Fold in the cherries, coconut, and chocolate. Drop tablespoon-size balls of dough onto a baking sheet. Bake for 10–12 minutes, until browned and cooked through.
5. Let cool for about 3 minutes, remove from the baking sheet, and cool completely before serving. Store in an airtight container for up to 1 week.

Nutrition:

Calories 136

Total fat 7 g.

Saturated fat 3 g.

Protein 4 g.

Carbohydrates 14 g.

Sugar 4 g.

Fiber 3 g.

Cholesterol 21 mg.

Sodium 11 mg.

Blueberry Breakfast Cake

Preparation time: 15 minutes

Cooking time: 45 minutes

Servings: 12

Ingredients:

For the Topping

- 1/4 c. finely chopped walnuts
- 1/2 tsp. ground cinnamon
- 2 tbsps butter, chopped into small pieces
- 2 tbsps sugar

For the Cake

- Nonstick cooking spray
- 1 c. whole-wheat pastry flour
- 1 c. oat flour
- 1/4 c. sugar
- 2 tsps. baking powder

- 1 large egg, beaten
- 1/2 c. skim milk
- 2 tbsps butter, melted
- 1 tsp. grated lemon peel
- 2 c. fresh or frozen blueberries

Directions:

To Make the Topping

1. In a small bowl, stir together the walnuts, cinnamon, butter, and sugar. Set aside.

To Make the Cake

1. Preheat the oven to 350 °F. Spray a 9-in. square pan with cooking spray. Set aside.
2. In a large bowl, stir together the pastry flour, oat flour, sugar, and baking powder.
3. Add the egg, milk, butter, and lemon peel, and stir until there are no dry spots.
4. Stir in the blueberries, and gently mix until incorporated. Press the batter into the prepared pan, using a spoon to flatten it into the dish.
5. Sprinkle the topping over the cake.

6. Bake for 40–45 minutes until a toothpick inserted into the cake comes out clean and serve.

Nutrition:

Calories 177

Total fat 7 g.

Saturated fat 3 g.

Protein 4 g.

Carbohydrates 26 g.

Sugar 9 g.

Fiber 3 g.

Cholesterol 26 mg.

Sodium 39 mg.

Whole-Grain Pancakes

Preparation time: 10 minutes

Cooking time: 15 minutes

Servings: 4–6

Ingredients:

- 2 c. whole-wheat pastry flour
- 4 tsps. baking powder
- 2 tsps. ground cinnamon
- 1/2 tsp. salt
- 2 c. skim milk, plus more as needed
- 2 large eggs
- 1 tbsp. honey
- Nonstick cooking spray

Maple syrup, for serving

Fresh fruit, for serving

Directions:

1. In a large bowl, stir together the flour, baking powder, cinnamon, and salt.

2. Add the milk, eggs, and honey, and stir well to combine. If needed, add more milk, 1 tbsp. at a time, until there are no dry spots and you have a pourable batter.
3. Heat a large skillet over medium-high heat, and spray it with cooking spray.
4. Using a 1/4-cup measuring cup, scoop 2 or 3 pancakes into the skillet at a time. Cook for a couple of minutes, until bubbles form on the surface of the pancakes, flip, and cook for 1–2 minutes more, until golden brown and cooked through. Repeat with the remaining batter.
5. Serve topped with maple syrup or fresh fruit.

Nutrition:

Calories 392

Total fat 4 g.

Saturated fat 1 g.

Protein 15 g.

Carbohydrates 71 g.

Sugar 11 g.

Fiber 9 g.

Cholesterol 95 mg.

Sodium 396 mg.

Buckwheat Grouts Breakfast Bowl

Preparation time: 5 minutes, plus overnight to soak

Cooking time: 10–12 minutes

Servings: 4

Ingredients:

- 3 c. skim milk
- 1 c. buckwheat grouts
- 1/4 c. chia seeds
- 2 tsps. vanilla extract
- 1/2 tsp. ground cinnamon
- Pinch salt
- 1 c. water
- 1/2 c. unsalted pistachios
- 2 c. sliced fresh strawberries
- 1/4 c. cacao nibs (optional)

Directions:
1. In a large bowl, stir together the milk, groats, chia seeds, vanilla, cinnamon, and salt. Cover and refrigerate overnight.
2. The next morning, transfer the soaked mixture to a medium pot and add the water. Bring to a boil over medium-high heat, reduce the heat to maintain a simmer, and cook for 10–12 minutes, until the buckwheat is tender and thickened.
3. Transfer to bowls and serve, topped with the pistachios, strawberries, and cacao nibs (if using).

Nutrition:

Calories 340

Total fat 8 g.

Saturated fat 1 g.

Protein 15 g.

Carbohydrates 52 g.

Sugar 14 g.

Fiber 10 g.

Cholesterol 4 mg.

Sodium 140 mg.

Peach Muesli Bake

Preparation time: 10 minutes

Cooking time: 40 minutes

Servings: 8

Ingredients:

- Nonstick cooking spray
- 2 c. skim milk
- 1 1/2 c. rolled oats
- 1/2 c. chopped walnuts
- 1 large egg
- 2 tbsps maple syrup
- 1 tsp. ground cinnamon
- 1 tsp. baking powder
- 1/2 tsp. salt
- 2–3 peaches, sliced

Directions:

1. Preheat the oven to 375 °F. Spray a 9-in. square baking dish with cooking spray. Set aside.
2. In a large bowl, stir together the milk, oats, walnuts, egg, maple syrup, cinnamon, baking powder, and salt. Spread half the mixture in the prepared baking dish.

3. Place half the peaches in a single layer across the oat mixture.
4. Spread the remaining oat mixture over the top. Add the remaining peaches in a thin layer over the oats. Bake for 35–40 minutes, uncovered until thickened and browned.
5. Cut into 8 squares and serve warm.

Nutrition:

Calories 138

Total fat 3 g.

Saturated fat 1 g.

Protein 6 g.

Carbohydrates 22 g.

Sugar 10 g.

Fiber 3 g.

Cholesterol 24 mg.

Sodium 191 mg.

Steel-Cut Oatmeal Bowl with Fruit and Nuts

Preparation time: 5 minutes

Cooking time: 20 minutes

Servings: 4

Ingredients:

- 1 c. steel-cut oats
- 2 c. almond milk
- 3/4 c. water
- 1 tsp. ground cinnamon
- 1/4 tsp. salt
- 2 c. chopped fresh fruit, such as blueberries, strawberries, raspberries, or peaches
- 1/2 c. chopped walnuts
- 1/4 c. chia seeds

Directions:

1. In a medium saucepan over medium-high heat, combine the oats, almond milk, water, cinnamon, and salt. Bring to a boil, reduce the heat to low, and simmer for 15–20 minutes, until the oats are softened and thickened.
2. Top each bowl with 1/2 c of fresh fruit, 2 tbsps of walnuts, and 1 tbsp of chia seeds before serving.

Nutrition:

Calories 288

Total fat 11 g.

Saturated fat 1 g.

Protein 10 g.

Carbohydrates 38 g.

Sugar 7 g.

Fiber 10 g.

Cholesterol 0 mg.

Sodium 329 mg.

Whole-Grain Dutch Baby Pancake

Preparation time: 5 minutes

Cooking time: 25 minutes

Servings: 4

Ingredients:

- 2 tbsps coconut oil
- 1/2 c. whole-wheat flour
- 1/4 c. skim milk
- 3 large eggs
- 1 tsp. vanilla extract
- 1/2 tsp. baking powder
- 1/4 tsp. salt
- 1/4 tsp. ground cinnamon
- Powdered sugar, for dusting

Directions:

1. Preheat the oven to 400 °F.
2. Put the coconut oil in a medium oven-safe skillet, and place the skillet in the oven to melt the oil while it preheats.

3. In a blender, combine the flour, milk, eggs, vanilla, baking powder, salt, and cinnamon. Process until smooth.
4. Carefully remove the skillet from the oven and tilt to spread the oil around evenly.
5. Pour the batter into the skillet and return it to the oven for 23–25 minutes, until the pancake puffs and lightly browns.
6. Remove, dust lightly with powdered sugar, cut into 4 wedges, and serve.

Nutrition:

Calories 195
Total fat 11 g.

Saturated fat 7 g.

Protein 8 g.

Carbohydrates 16 g.

Sugar 1 g.

Fiber 2 g.

Cholesterol 140 mg.

Sodium 209 mg.

Mushroom, Zucchini and Onion Frittata

Preparation time: 10 minutes

Cooking time: 20 minutes

Servings: 4

Ingredients:

- 1 tbsp. extra-virgin olive oil
- 1/2 onion, chopped
- 1 medium zucchini, chopped
- 1 1/2 c. sliced mushrooms
- 6 large eggs, beaten
- 2 tbsps skim milk
- Salt
- Freshly ground black pepper
- 1-oz. feta cheese, crumbled

Directions:

1. Preheat the oven to 400 °F.
2. In a medium oven-safe skillet over medium-high heat, heat the olive oil.

3. Add the onion and sauté for 3–5 minutes, until translucent.
4. Add the zucchini and mushrooms, and cook for 3–5 more minutes, until the vegetables are tender.
5. Meanwhile, in a small bowl, whisk the eggs, milk, salt, and pepper. Pour the mixture into the skillet, stirring to combine, and transfer the skillet to the oven. Cook for 7–9 minutes, until set.
6. Sprinkle with the feta cheese, and cook for 1–2 minutes more, until heated through.
7. Remove, cut into 4 wedges, and serve.

Nutrition:

Calories 178

Total fat 13 g.

Saturated fat 4 g.

Protein 12 g.

Carbohydrates 5 g.

Sugar 3 g.

Fiber 1 g.

Cholesterol 285 mg.

Sodium 234 mg.

Spinach and Cheese Quiche

Preparation time: 10 minutes, plus 10 minutes to rest

Cooking time: 50 minutes

Servings: 4–6

Ingredients:

- Nonstick cooking spray
- 1 tbsp. + 2 tsps. extra-virgin olive oil, divided
- 1/2 tsp. salt
- Freshly ground black pepper
- 1 onion, finely chopped
- 1 (10-oz.) bag fresh spinach
- 4 large eggs
- 1/2 c. skim milk
- 1-oz. Gruyere cheese, shredded

Directions:

1. Preheat the oven to 350 °F. Spray a 9-in. pie dish with cooking spray.
   Set aside.
2. In a large skillet over medium-high heat, heat olive oil.
3. Add the onion and sauté for 3–5 minutes, until softened.

4. By handfuls, add the spinach, stirring between each addition, until it just starts to wilt before adding more. Cook for about 1 minute, until it cooks down.
5. In a medium bowl, whisk the eggs and milk. Add the gruyere, and season with salt and some pepper. Fold the eggs into the spinach. Pour the mixture into the pie dish and bake for 25 minutes, until the eggs are set.
6. Let rest for 10 minutes before serving.

Nutrition:

Calories 445

Total fat 14 g.

Saturated fat 4 g.

Protein 19 g.

Carbohydrates 68 g.

Sugar 6 g.

Fiber 7 g.

Cholesterol 193 mg.

Sodium 773 mg.

Spicy Jalapeno Popper Deviled Eggs

Preparation time: 5 minutes

Cooking time: 5 minutes

Servings: 4

Ingredients:

- 4 large whole eggs, hardboiled
- 2 tbsps keto-friendly mayonnaise
- 1/4 c. cheddar cheese, grated
- 2 slices bacon, cooked and crumbled
- 1 jalapeno, sliced

Directions:

1. Cut eggs in half, remove the yolk, and put them in a bowl.
2. Lay egg whites on a platter.
3. Mix in the remaining ingredients and mash them with the egg yolks.
4. Transfer the yolk mixture back to the egg whites.

Nutrition:

Calories 176

Fat 14 g.

Carbohydrates 0.7 g.

Protein 10 g.

Lovely Porridge

Preparation time: 15 minutes

Cooking time: Nil

Servings: 2

Ingredients:

- 2 tbsps coconut flour
- 2 tbsps vanilla protein powder
- 3 tbsps Golden Flaxseed meal
- 1/2 c. almond milk, unsweetened
- Powdered erythritol

Directions:

1. Take a bowl and mix with flaxseed meal, protein powder, coconut flour, and mix well.
2. Add the mix to the saucepan (placed over medium heat).
3. Add almond milk and stir, let the mixture thicken.
4. Add your desired amount of sweetener and serve.
5. Enjoy!

Nutrition:

Calories 259

Fat 13 g.

Carbohydrates 5 g.

Protein 16 g.

Salty Macadamia Chocolate Smoothie

Preparation time: 5 minutes

Cooking time: Nil

Servings: 1

Ingredients:

- 2 tbsps macadamia nuts, salted
- 1/3 c. chocolate whey protein powder, low carb
- 1 c. almond milk, unsweetened

Directions:

1. Add the listed ingredients to your blender and blend until you have a smooth mixture.
2. Chill and enjoy it!

Nutrition:

Calories 165

Fat 2 g.

Carbohydrates 1 g.

Protein 12 g.

Basil and Tomato Baked Eggs

Preparation time: 10 minutes

Cooking time: 15 minutes

Servings: 4

Ingredients:

- 1 garlic clove, minced
- 1 c. canned tomatoes
- 1/4 c. fresh basil leaves, roughly chopped
- 1/2 tsp. chili powder
- 1 tbsp. olive oil
- 4 whole eggs
- Salt and pepper to taste

Directions:

1. Preheat your oven to 375 °F.
2. Take a small baking dish and grease it with olive oil.

3. Add garlic, basil, tomatoes, chili, olive oil into a dish and stir.
4. Crackdown eggs into a dish, keeping space between the two.
5. Sprinkle the whole dish with salt and pepper.
6. Place in oven and cook for 12 minutes until eggs are set and tomatoes are bubbling.
7. Serve with basil on top.
8. Enjoy!

Nutrition:

Calories 235

Fat 16 g.

Carbohydrates 7 g.

Protein 14 g.

Cinnamon and Coconut Porridge

Preparation time: 5 minutes

Cooking time: 5 minutes

Servings: 4

Ingredients:

- 2 c of water
- 1 c. 36 % heavy cream
- 1/2 c. unsweetened dried coconut, shredded
- 2 tbsps flaxseed meal
- 1 tbsp. butter
- 1 and 1/2 tsp. stevia
- 1 tsp. cinnamon
- Salt to taste
- Toppings as blueberries

Directions:

1. Add the listed ingredients to a small pot, mix well.
2. Transfer the pot to a stove and place it over medium-low heat.
3. Bring the mix to a slow boil.
4. Stir well and remove the heat.
5. Divide the mix into equal servings and let them sit for 10 minutes.

6. Top with your desired toppings and enjoy!

Nutrition:

Calories 171

Fat 16 g.

Carbohydrates 6 g.

Protein 2 g.

An Omelet of Swiss Chard

Preparation time: 5 minutes

Cooking time: 5 minutes

Servings: 4

Ingredients:

- 4 eggs, lightly beaten
- 4 c. Swiss chard, sliced
- 2 tbsps butter
- 1/2 tsp. garlic salt
- Fresh pepper

Directions:

1. Take a non-stick frying pan and place it over medium-low heat.
2. Once the butter melts, add Swiss chard and stir cook for 2 minutes.
3. Pour egg into the pan and gently stir them into the Swiss chard.
4. Season with garlic salt and pepper.
5. Cook for 2 minutes.
6. Serve and enjoy!

Nutrition:

Calories 260

Fat 21 g.

Carbohydrates 4 g.

Protein 14 g.

Cheesy Low-Carb Omelet

Preparation time: 5 minutes

Cooking time: 5 minutes

Servings: 5

Ingredients:

- 2 whole eggs
- 1 tbsp. water
- 1 tbsp. butter
- 3 thin slices of salami
- 5 fresh basil leaves
- 5 thin slices, fresh ripe tomatoes
- 2 oz. fresh mozzarella cheese
- Salt and pepper as needed

Directions:

1. Take a small bowl and whisk in eggs and water.
2. Take a non-stick pan and place it over medium heat, add the butter and let it melt.
3. Pour egg mixture and cook for 30 seconds.
4. Spread salami slices on half of the egg mix and top with cheese, tomatoes, basil slices.
5. Season with salt and pepper according to your taste.

6. Cook for 2 minutes and fold the egg with the empty half.
7. Cover and cook on low for 1 minute.
8. Serve and enjoy!

Nutrition:

Calories 451

Fat 36 g.

Carbohydrates 3 g.

Protein: 33 g.

Bacon and Chicken Garlic Wrap

Preparation time: 15 minutes

Cooking time: 10 minutes

Servings: 4

Ingredients:

- 1 chicken fillet, cut into small cubes
- 8–9 thin slices of bacon, cut into small cubes
- 6 garlic cloves, minced

Directions:

1. Preheat your oven to 400 °F.
2. Line a baking tray with aluminum foil.
3. Add minced garlic to a bowl and rub each chicken piece with it.
4. Wrap bacon piece around each garlic chicken bite.
5. Secure with a toothpick.
6. Transfer bites to the baking sheet, keeping a little bit of space between them.
7. Bake for about 15–20 minutes until crispy.
8. Serve and enjoy!

Nutrition:

Calories 260

Fat 19 g.

Carbohydrates 5 g.

Protein 22 g.

Grilled Chicken Platter

Preparation time: 5 minutes

Cooking time: 10 minutes

Servings: 6

Ingredients:

- 3 large chicken breasts, sliced half lengthwise
- 10-oz. spinach, frozen and drained
- 3-oz. mozzarella cheese, part-skim
- 1/2 a cup of roasted red peppers, cut in long strips
- 1 tsp of olive oil
- 2 garlic cloves, minced
- Salt and pepper as needed

Directions:

1. Preheat your oven to 400 °F.
2. Slice 3 chicken breast lengthwise.
3. Take a non-stick pan and grease with cooking spray.
4. Bake for 2–3 minutes on each side.

5. Take another skillet and cook spinach and garlic in oil for 3 minutes.
6. Place chicken on an oven pan and top with spinach, roasted peppers, and mozzarella.
7. Bake until the cheese melt

Nutrition:

Calories 195

Fat 7 g.

Net carbohydrates 3 g.

Protein 30 g.

Parsley Chicken Breast

Preparation time: 10 minutes

Cooking time: 40 minutes

Servings: 4

Ingredients:

- 1 tbsp. dry parsley
- 1 tbsp. dry basil
- 4 chicken breast halves, boneless and skinless

- 1/2 tsp. salt
- 1/2 tsp. red pepper flakes, crushed
- 2 tomatoes, sliced

Directions:

1. Preheat your oven to 350 °F.
2. Take a 9x13 in. baking dish and grease it up with cooking spray.
3. Sprinkle 1 tbsp of parsley, 1 tsp of basil, and spread the mixture over your baking dish.
4. Arrange the chicken breast halves over the dish and sprinkle garlic slices on top.
5. Take a small bowl and add 1 tsp. parsley, 1 tsp of basil, salt, basil, red pepper and mix well. Pour the mixture over the chicken breast.
6. Top with tomato slices and cover; bake for 25 minutes.
7. Remove the cover and bake for 15 more minutes.

Nutrition:

Calories 150

Fat 4 g.

Carbohydrates 4 g.

Protein 25 g.

Mustard Chicken

Preparation time: 10 minutes

Cooking time: 40 minutes

Servings: 4

Ingredients:

- 4 chicken breasts
- 1/2 c. chicken broth
- 3–4 tbsps mustard
- 3 tbsps olive oil
- 1 tsp. paprika
- 1 tsp. chili powder
- 1 tsp. garlic powder

Directions:

1. Take a small bowl and mix mustard, olive oil, paprika, garlic powder, chicken broth, and chili.
2. Add chicken breast and marinate for 30 minutes.
3. Take a lined baking sheet and arrange the chicken.
4. Bake for 35 minutes at 375 °F.
5. Serve and enjoy!

Nutrition:

Calories 531

Fat 23 g.

Carbohydrates 10 g.

Protein 64 g.

Balsamic Chicken

Preparation time: 10 minutes

Cooking time: 25 minutes

Servings: 6

Ingredients:

- 6 chicken breast halves, skinless and boneless
- 1 tsp. garlic salt
- Ground black pepper
- 2 tbsps olive oil
- 1 onion, thinly sliced
- 14- and 1/2-oz. tomatoes, diced
- 1/2 c. balsamic vinegar
- 1 tsp. dried basil
- 1 tsp. dried oregano
- 1 tsp. dried rosemary
- 1/2 tsp. dried thyme

Directions:

1. Season both sides of your chicken breasts thoroughly with pepper and garlic salt.
2. Take a skillet and place it over medium heat.

3. Add some oil and cook your seasoned chicken for 3–4 minutes per side until the breasts are nicely browned.
4. Add the onion and cook for another 3–4 minutes until the onion is browned.
5. Pour the diced-up tomatoes and balsamic vinegar over your chicken and season with some rosemary, basil, thyme, and oregano.
6. Simmer the chicken for about 15 minutes until they are no longer pink.
7. Take an instant-read thermometer and check if the internal temperature gives a reading of 165 °F.
8. If yes, then you are good to go!

Nutrition:

Calories 196 Fat 7 g.

Carbohydrates 7 g.

Protein 23 g.

Greek Chicken Breast

Preparation time: 10 minutes

Cooking time: 25 minutes

Servings: 4

Ingredients:

- 4 chicken breast halves, skinless, and boneless
- 1 c. extra-virgin olive oil
- 1 lemon, juiced
- 2 tsps. garlic, crushed
- 1/2 tsps. black pepper
- 1/3 tsp. paprika
- Salt, to taste

Directions:

1. Cut 3 slits in the chicken breast.
2. Take a small bowl and whisk in olive oil, salt, lemon juice, garlic, paprika, pepper, and whisk for 30 seconds

3. Place chicken in a large bowl and pour the marinade
4. Rub the marinade all over using your hands
5. Refrigerate overnight
6. Pre-heat grill to medium heat and oil the grate
7. Cook chicken in the grill until the center is no longer pink
8. Serve and enjoy!

Nutrition:

Calories 644

Fat 57 g.

Carbohydrates 2 g.

Protein 27 g.

Chipotle Lettuce Chicken

Preparation time: 10 minutes

Cooking time: 25 minutes

Servings: 6

Ingredients:

- 1 lb. chicken breast, cut into strips
- Splash of olive oil
- 1 red onion, finely sliced
- 14 oz. tomatoes
- 1 tsp. chipotle, chopped
- 1/2 tsp. cumin
- Pinch of sugar
- Lettuce as needed
- Fresh coriander leaves
- Jalapeno chilies, sliced
- Fresh tomato slices for garnish
- Lemon wedges

Directions:

1. Take a non-stick frying pan and place it over medium heat.
2. Add oil and heat it up.

3. Add chicken and cook until brown.
4. Keep the chicken on the side.
5. Add tomatoes, sugar, chipotle, cumin to the same pan and simmer for 25 minutes until you have a nice sauce.
6. Add the chicken into the sauce and cook for 5 minutes.
7. Transfer the mix to another place.
8. Use the lettuce wraps to take a portion of the mixture and serve with lemon wedges, tomato slices, coriander, and jalapeno.
9. Enjoy!

Nutrition:

Calories 332 Fat 15 g.

Carbohydrates 13 g.

Protein 34 g.

Lunch

Grilled Tempeh with Pineapple

Preparation time: 12 minutes

Cooking time: 16 minutes

Servings: 3

Ingredients:

- 10 oz. tempeh, sliced
- 1 red bell pepper, quartered
- 1/4 pineapple, sliced into rings
- 6 oz. green beans
- 1 tbsp. coconut aminos
- 1/2 tbsp. orange juice, freshly squeeze
- 1/2 tbsp. lemon juice, freshly squeezed
- 1 tbsp. extra-virgin olive oil
- 1/4 c. hoisin sauce

Directions:

1. Blend together the olive oil, orange and lemon juices, coconut aminos or soy sauce, and hoisin sauce in a bowl. Add the diced tempeh and set aside.
2. Heat up the grill or place a grill pan over a medium-high flame. Once hot, lift the marinated tempeh from the bowl with a pair of tongs and transfer them to the grill or pan.
3. Grille for 2–3 minutes, or until browned all over.
4. Grill the sliced pineapples alongside the tempeh, then transfer them directly onto the serving platter.
5. Place the grilled tempeh beside the grilled pineapple and cover with aluminum foil to keep warm.
6. Meanwhile, place the green beans and bell peppers in a bowl and add just enough of the marinade to coat.
7. Prepare the grill pan and add the vegetables. Grill until fork tender and slightly charred.

8. Transfer the grilled vegetables to the serving platter and arrange artfully with the tempeh and pineapple. Serve at once.

Nutrition:

Calories 163

Total fat 4.2 g.

Saturated fat 0.8 g.

Cholesterol 0 mg.

Sodium 861 mg.

Total carbs 22.5 g.

Fiber 6.3 g.

Sugar 2.3 g.

Protein 9.2 g.

Courgettes in Cider Sauce

Preparation time: 13 minutes

Cooking time: 17 minutes

Servings: 3

Ingredients:

- 2 c. baby courgettes
- 3 tbsps vegetable stock
- 2 tbsps apple cider vinegar
- 1 tbsp. light brown sugar
- 4 spring onions, finely sliced
- 1-piece fresh ginger root, grated
- The rind of 1 lemon
- Juice of 1 lemon
- The rind of 1 orange
- Juice of 1 orange
- 1 tsp. cornflour
- 2 tsps. Water

Directions:

1. Bring a pan with salted water to a boil. Add courgettes. Bring to a boil for 5 minutes.
2. Meanwhile, in a pan, combine vegetable stock, apple cider vinegar, brown sugar, onions, ginger root, lemon juice and rind, and orange juice and rind. Take to a boil. Lower the heat and allow simmering for 3 minutes.
3. Mix the cornflour with water. Stir well. Pour into the sauce. Continue stirring until the sauce thickens.
4. Drain courgettes. Transfer to the serving dish. Spoon over the sauce. Toss to coat courgettes. Serve.

Nutrition:

Calories 173
Total fat 9.2 g.
Saturated fat 0.8 g.
Cholesterol 0 mg.
Sodium 861 mg.
Total carbs 22.5 g.

Fiber 6.3 g.

Sugar 2.3 g.

Protein 9.2 g.

Baked Mixed Mushrooms

Preparation time: 8 minutes

Cooking time: 20 minutes

Servings: 3

Ingredients:

- 2 c. mixed wild mushrooms
- 1 c. chestnut mushrooms
- 2 c. dried porcini
- 2 shallots
- 4 garlic cloves
- 3 c. raw pecans
- 1/2 bunch fresh thyme
- 1 bunch flat-leaf parsley
- 2 tbsps olive oil
- 2 fresh bay leaves

- 1/2 c. stale bread
- Pinch of black pepper and sea salt

Directions:

1. Remove skin and finely chop garlic and shallots. Roughly chop the wild mushrooms and chestnut mushrooms. Pick the leaves of the thyme and tear the bread into small pieces. Put inside the pressure cooker.
2. Place the pecans and roughly chop the nuts. Pick the parsley leaves and roughly chop.
3. Place the porcini in a bowl then add 300 ml of boiling water. Set aside until needed.
4. Heat oil in the pressure cooker. Add the garlic and shallots. Cook for 3 minutes while stirring occasionally.
5. Drain porcini and reserve the liquid. Add the porcini into the pressure cooker together with the wild mushrooms and chestnut mushrooms. Add the bay leaves and thyme.

6. Position the lid and lock it in place. Put to high heat and bring to high pressure. Adjust heat to stabilize. Cook for 10 minutes.

    Adjust taste if necessary.

7. Transfer the mushroom mixture into a bowl and set aside to cool completely.

8. Once the mushrooms are completely cool, add the bread, pecans, a pinch of black pepper and sea salt, and half of the reserved liquid into the bowl. Mix well. Add more reserved liquid if the mixture seems dry.

9. Add more than half of the parsley into the bowl and stir. Transfer the mixture into a 20x25 cm. lightly greased baking dish and cover with tin foil.

10. Bake in the oven for 35 minutes. Then, get rid of the foil and cook for another 10 minutes. Once done, sprinkle the remaining parsley on top and serve with bread or crackers.

Nutrition:

Calories 343

Total fat 4.2 g.

Saturated fat 0.8 g.

Cholesterol 0 mg.

Sodium 861 mg.

Total carbs 22.5 g.

Fiber 6.3 g.

Sugar 2.3 g.

Protein 9.2 g.

Spiced Okra

Preparation time: 14 minutes
Cooking time: 16 minutes
Servings: 3
Ingredients:

- 2 c. okra
- 1/4 tsp. stevia

- 1 tsp. chili powder
- 1/2 teaspoon ground turmeric
- 1 tbsp. ground coriander
- 2 tbsps fresh coriander, chopped
- 1 tbsp. ground cumin
- 1/4 tsp. salt
- 1 tbsp. desiccated coconut
- 3 vegetable oil
- 1/2 teaspoon black mustard seeds
- 1/2 teaspoon cumin seeds
- Fresh tomatoes, to garnish

Directions:

1. Trim the okra. Wash and dry.
2. Combine stevia, chili powder, turmeric, ground coriander, fresh coriander, cumin, salt, and desiccated coconut in a bowl.

3. Heat the oil in a pan. Cook mustard and cumin seeds for 3 minutes. Stir continuously. Add okra. Tip in the spice mixture. Cook on low heat for 8 minutes.
4. Transfer to a serving dish. Garnish with fresh tomatoes.

Nutrition:

Calories 163

Total fat 4.2 g.

Saturated fat 0.8 g.

Cholesterol 0 mg.

Sodium 861 mg.

Total carbs 22.5 g.

Fiber 6.3 g.

Sugar 2.3 g.

Protein 9.2 g.

Lemony Salmon Burgers

Preparation time: 10 minutes

Cooking time: 10 minutes

Servings: 4

Ingredients:

- 2 (3-oz) cans boneless, skinless pink salmon
- 1/4 c. panko breadcrumbs
- 4 tsp. lemon juice
- 1/4 c. red bell pepper
- 1/4 c. sugar-free yogurt
- 1 egg
- 2 (1.5-oz) whole wheat hamburger toasted buns

Directions:

1. Mix drained and flaked salmon, finely-chopped bell pepper, panko breadcrumbs.
2. Combine 2 tbsp. sugar-free yogurt, 3 tsp. fresh lemon juice, and egg in a bowl. Shape mixture into 2 (3-in.) patties, bake on the skillet over medium heat for 4–5 minutes per side.

3. Stir together 2 tbsp. sugar-free yogurt and 1 tsp. lemon juice; spread over bottom halves of buns.
4. Top each with 1 patty, and cover with bun tops.

This dish is very mouth-watering!

Nutrition:

Calories 131

Protein 12 g.

Fat 1 g.

Carbohydrates 19 g.

Caprese Turkey Burgers

Preparation time: 10 minutes

Cooking time: 10 minutes

Servings: 4

Ingredients:

- 1/2 lb. 93 % lean ground turkey
- 2 (1.5-oz) whole-wheat hamburger buns (toasted)

- 1/4 c. shredded mozzarella cheese (part-skim)
- 1 egg
- 1 big tomato
- 1 small clove garlic
- 4 large basil leaves
- 1/8 tsp. salt
- 1/8 tsp. pepper

Directions:

1. Mix turkey, white egg, minced garlic, salt, and pepper until combined.
2. Shape into 2 cutlets. Put the cutlets into a skillet; cook for 5–7 minutes per side.
3. Top cutlets properly with cheese and sliced tomato at the end of cooking.
4. Put 1 cutlet on the bottom of each bun.
5. Top each patty with 2 basil leaves. Cover with bun tops.

Nutrition:

Calories 180

Protein 7 g.

Fat 4 g.

Carbohydrates 20 g.

Pasta Salad

Preparation time: 15 minutes
Cooking time: 15 minutes
Servings: 4
Ingredients:

- 8 oz. whole-wheat pasta
- 2 tomatoes
- 1 (5-oz) pkg. spring mix
- 9 slices bacon
- 1/3 c. mayonnaise (reduced-fat)

- 1 tbsp. Dijon mustard
- 3 tbsp. apple cider vinegar
- 1/4 tsp. salt
- 1/2 tsp. pepper

Directions:

1. Cook pasta.
2. Chilled pasta, chopped tomatoes, and spring mix in a bowl.
3. Crumble cooked bacon over pasta.
4. Combine mayonnaise, mustard, vinegar, salt, and pepper in a small bowl.
5. Pour dressing over pasta, stirring to coat.

Understanding diabetes is the first step in curing.

Nutrition:

Calories 200

Protein 15 g.

Fat 3 g.

Carbohydrates 6 g.

Chicken, Strawberry, and Avocado Salad

Preparation time: 10 minutes
Cooking time: 5 minutes
Servings: 4
Ingredients:

- 1.5 c. chicken (skin removed)
- 1/4 c. almonds
- 2 (5-oz) pkg. salad greens
- 1 (16-oz) pkg. strawberries
- 1 avocado
- 1/4 c. green onion
- 1/4 c. lime juice
- 3 tbsp. extra-virgin olive oil
- 2 tbsp. honey
- 1/4 tsp. salt
- 1/4 tsp. pepper

Directions:

1. Toast almonds until golden and fragrant.
2. Mix lime juice, oil, honey, salt, and pepper.
3. Mix greens, sliced strawberries, chicken, diced avocado, and sliced green onion, and sliced almonds; drizzle with dressing. Toss to coat.

Nutrition:

Calories 150

Protein 15 g.

Fat 10 g.

Carbohydrates 5 g.

Lemon-Thyme Eggs

Preparation time: 10 minutes

Cooking time: 5 minutes

Servings: 4

Ingredients:

- 7 large eggs
- 1/4 c. mayonnaise (reduced-fat)
- 2 tsp. lemon juice
- 1 tsp. Dijon mustard
- 1 tsp. chopped fresh thyme
- 1/8 tsp. cayenne pepper

Directions:

1. Bring eggs to a boil.
2. Peel and cut each egg in half lengthwise.
3. Remove the yolks to a bowl. Add mayonnaise, lemon juice, mustard, thyme, and cayenne to the egg yolks; mash to blend. Fill the egg white halves with the yolk mixture.
4. Chill until ready to serve.

Nutrition:

Calories 40

Protein 10 g.

Fat 6 g.

Carbohydrates 2 g.

Spinach Salad with Bacon

Preparation time: 15 minutes
Cooking time: 0 minutes
Servings: 4
Ingredients:

- 8 slices center-cut bacon
- 3 tbsp. extra-virgin olive oil
- 1 (5-oz) pkg. baby spinach
- 1 tbsp. apple cider vinegar
- 1 tsp. Dijon mustard
- 1/2 tsp. honey
- 1/4 tsp. salt
- 1/2 tsp. Pepper

Directions:

1. Mix vinegar, mustard, honey, salt, and pepper in a bowl.

2. Whisk in oil. Place spinach in a serving bowl; drizzle with dressing, and toss to coat.
3. Sprinkle with cooked and crumbled bacon.

Nutrition:

Calories 110

Protein 6 g.

Fat 2 g.

Carbohydrates 1 g.

Cauliflower Rice with Chicken

Preparation time: 15 minutes
Cooking time: 15 minutes
Servings: 4

Ingredients:

- 1/2 large cauliflower
- 3/4 c. cooked meat
- 1/2 bell pepper

- 1 carrot
- 2 ribs celery
- 1 tbsp. stir fry sauce (low carb)
- 1 tbsp. extra-virgin olive oil
- Salt and pepper to taste

Directions:

1. Chop cauliflower in a processor to "rice." Place in a bowl.
2. Properly chop all vegetables in a food processor into thin slices.
3. Add cauliflower and other plants to a wok with heated oil. Fry until all veggies are tender.
4. Add chopped meat and sauce to the wok and fry for 10 minutes.

Nutrition:

Calories 200

Protein 10 g.

Fat 12 g.

Carbohydrates 10 g.

Turkey with Fried Eggs

Preparation time: 10 minutes

Cooking time: 20 minutes

Servings: 4

Ingredients:

- 1 cooked turkey thigh
- 1 large onion (about 2 c. diced)
- Butter
- Chile flakes
- 4 eggs
- Salt to taste
- Pepper to taste

Directions:

1. Dice the turkey.
2. Cook the onion in as much unsalted butter as you feel comfortable with until it's fragrant and translucent.
3. Add 1 c of diced cooked turkey, salt, and pepper to taste, and cook for 20 minutes.
4. Top each with a fried egg.

Nutrition:

Calories 170

Protein 19 g.

Fat 7 g.

Carbohydrates 6 g.

Kale and White Bean Stew

Preparation time: 15 minutes

Cooking time: 25 minutes

Servings: 4

Ingredients:

- 1 (15-oz.) can low-sodium cannellini beans, rinsed and drained, divided
- 1 tbsp. olive oil
- 1 medium onion, chopped
- 2 garlic cloves, minced
- 2 celery stalks, chopped
- 3 medium carrots, chopped

- 2 c. low-sodium vegetable broth
- 1 tsp. apple cider vinegar
- 2 c. chopped kale
- 1 c. shelled edamame
- 1/4 c. quinoa
- 1 tsp. dried thyme
- 1/2 tsp. cayenne pepper
- 1/2 tsp. salt
- 1/4 tsp. freshly ground black pepper

Directions:

1. Put half the beans into a blender and blend until smooth. Set aside.
2. In a large soup pot over medium heat, heat the oil. When the oil is shining, include the onion and garlic, and cook until the onion softens and the garlic is sweet, for about 3 minutes. Add the celery and carrots, and continue cooking until the vegetables soften, for about 5 minutes.
3. Add the broth, vinegar, unblended beans, kale, edamame, and quinoa, and bring the mixture to a

boil. Reduce the heat and simmer until the vegetables soften, for about 10 minutes.

4. Add the blended beans, thyme, cayenne, salt, and black pepper, increase the heat to medium-high, and bring the mixture to a boil. Reduce the heat and simmer, uncovered, until the flavors combine, for about 5 minutes.

5. Into each of 4 containers, scoop 1 3/4 cups of stew.

Nutrition:

Calories 373

Total fat 7 g.

Saturated fat 1 g.

Protein 15 g.

Total carbs 65 g.

Fiber 15 g.

Sugar 13 g.

Sodium 540 mg.

Slow Cooker Two-Bean Sloppy Joes

Preparation time: 10 minutes

Cooking time: 6 hours

Servings: 4

Ingredients:

- 1 (15-oz.) can of low-sodium black beans
- 1 (15-oz.) can of low-sodium pinto beans
- 1 (15-oz.) can of no-salt-added diced tomatoes
- 1 medium green bell pepper, cored, seeded, and chopped
- 1 medium yellow onion, chopped
- 1/4 c. low-sodium vegetable broth
- 2 garlic cloves, minced
- 2 servings (1/4 c.) meal prep barbecue sauce or bottled barbecue sauce
- 1/4 tsp. salt
- 1/4 tsp. freshly ground black pepper
- whole-wheat buns

Directions:

1. In a slow cooker, combine the black beans, pinto beans, diced tomatoes, bell pepper, onion, broth, garlic, meal prep barbecue sauce, salt, and black pepper. Stir the ingredients, then cover and cook on low for 6 hours.
2. Into each of 4 containers, spoon 1 1/4 c of sloppy joe mix. Serve with 1 whole-wheat bun.
3. Storage: place airtight containers in the refrigerator for up to 1 week. To freeze, place freezer-safe containers in the freezer for up to 2 months. To defrost, refrigerate overnight. To reheat individual portions, microwave uncovered on high for 2–2 1/2 minutes. Alternatively, reheat the entire dish in a saucepan on the stovetop. Bring the sloppy joes to a boil, then reduce the heat and simmer until heated through, for 10–15 minutes. Serve with a whole-wheat bun.

Nutrition:

Calories 392

Total fat 3 g.

Saturated fat 0 g.

Protein 17 g.

Total carbs 79 g.

Fiber 19 g.

Sugar 15 g.

Sodium 759 mg.

Lighter Eggplant Parmesan

Preparation time: 15 minutes
Cooking time: 35 minutes
Servings: 4

Ingredients:

- Nonstick cooking spray
- 3 eggs, beaten
- 1 tbsp. dried parsley

- 2 tsps. ground oregano
- 1/8 tsp. freshly ground black pepper
- 1 c. panko bread crumbs, preferably whole-wheat
- 1 large eggplant (about 2 lbs.)
- 5 servings (2 1/2 c.) chunky tomato sauce or jarred low-sodium tomato sauce
- 1 c. part-skim mozzarella cheese
- 1/4 c. grated parmesan cheese

Directions:

1. Preheat the oven to 450 °F. Coat a baking sheet with cooking spray.
2. In a medium bowl, whisk together the eggs, parsley, oregano, and pepper.
3. Pour the panko into a separate medium bowl.
4. Slice the eggplant into 1/4-in.-thick slices. Dip each slice of eggplant into the egg mixture, shaking off the excess. Then dredge both sides of the eggplant in the panko bread crumbs. Place the coated eggplant on the prepared baking sheet, leaving a 1/2-in. space between each slice.

5. Bake for about 15 minutes until soft and golden brown. Remove from the oven and set aside to slightly cool.
6. Pour 1/2 c of chunky tomato sauce on the bottom of an 8-by-15-in. baking dish. Using a spatula or the back of a spoon spread the tomato sauce evenly. Place half the slices of the cooked eggplant, slightly overlapping, in the dish, and top with 1 c of chunky tomato sauce, 1/2 c of mozzarella, and 2 tbsps of grated parmesan. Repeat
the layer, ending with the cheese.
7. Bake uncovered for 20 minutes until the cheese is bubbling and slightly browned.
8. Remove from the oven and allow cooling for 15 minutes before dividing the eggplant equally into 4 separate containers.

Nutrition:

Calories 333

Total fat 14 g.

Saturated fat 6 g.

Protein 20 g.

Total carbs 35 g.

Fiber 11 g.

Sugar 15 g.

Sodium 994 mg.

Coconut-Lentil Curry

Preparation time: 15 minutes

Cooking time: 35 minutes

Servings: 4

Ingredients:

- 1 tbsp. olive oil
- 1 medium yellow onion, chopped
- 1 garlic clove, minced
- 1 medium red bell pepper, diced
- 1 (15-oz.) can green or brown lentils, rinsed and drained
- 1 (15-oz.) can no-salt-added diced tomatoes
- 2 tbsps tomato paste

- 4 tsps. curry powder
- 1/8 tsp. ground cloves
- 1 (15-oz.) can light coconut milk
- 1/4 tsp. salt
- 2 pieces' whole-wheat naan bread, halved, or 4 slices crusty bread

Directions:

1. In a large saucepan over medium heat, heat the olive oil. When the oil is shimmering, add both the onion and garlic and cook until the onion softens and the garlic is sweet, for about 3 minutes.
2. Add the bell pepper and continue cooking until it softens, about 5 minutes more. Add the lentils, tomatoes, tomato paste, curry powder, and cloves, and bring the mixture to a boil. Reduce the heat to medium-low, cover, and simmer
3. Add the coconut milk and salt, and return to a boil. Reduce the heat and simmer until the flavors combine, for about 5 minutes.
4. Into each of 4 containers, spoon 2 c of curry.

5. Enjoy each serving with half of a piece of naan bread or 1 slice of crusty bread.

Nutrition:

Calories 559

Total fat 16 g.

Saturated fat 7 g.

Protein 16 g.

Total carbs 86 g.

Fiber 16 g.

Sugar 18 g.

Sodium 819 mg.

Stuffed Portobello with Cheese

Preparation time: 15 minutes

Cooking time: 25 minutes

Servings: 4

Ingredients:

- 4 portobello mushroom caps
- 1 tbsp. olive oil
- 1/2 tsp. salt, divided
- 1/4 tsp. freshly ground black pepper, divided
- 1 c. baby spinach, chopped
- 1 1/2 c. part-skim ricotta cheese
- 1/2 c. part-skim shredded mozzarella cheese
- 1/4 c. grated parmesan cheese
- 1 garlic clove, minced
- 1 tbsp. dried parsley
- 2 tsps. dried oregano
- 4 tsps. unseasoned bread crumbs, divided
- 4 servings (4 c.) roasted broccoli with shallots

Directions:

1. Preheat the oven to 375 °F. Line a baking sheet with aluminum foil.
2. Brush the mushroom caps with olive oil, and sprinkle with 1/4 tsp. salt and 1/8 tsp. pepper. Put

the mushroom caps on the prepared baking sheet and bake until soft, about 12 minutes.

3. In a medium bowl, mix together the spinach, ricotta, mozzarella, parmesan, garlic, parsley, oregano, and the remaining 1/4 tsp of salt and 1/8 tsp of pepper.

4. Spoon 1/2 c of cheese mixture into each mushroom cap, and sprinkle each with 1 tsp of bread crumbs. Return the mushrooms to the oven for an additional 8–10 minutes until warmed through.

5. Remove from the oven and allow the mushrooms to cool for about 10 minutes before placing each in an individual container. Add 1 c of roasted broccoli with shallots to each container.

Nutrition:

Calories 419

Total fat 30 g.

Saturated fat 10 g.

Protein 23 g.

Total carbs 19 g.

Fiber 2 g.

Sugar 3 g.

Sodium 790 mg.

Lighter Shrimp Scampi

Preparation time: 15 minutes

Cooking time: 15 minutes

Servings: 4

Ingredients:

- 1/2 lbs. large peeled and deveined shrimp
- 1/4 tsp. salt
- 1/8 tsp. freshly ground black pepper
- 2 tbsps olive oil
- 1 shallot, chopped
- 2 garlic cloves, minced
- 1/4 c. cooking white wine
- Juice of 1/2 lemon (1 tbsp.)
- 1/2 tsp. sriracha
- 2 tbsps unsalted butter, at room temperature
- 1/4 c. chopped fresh parsley
- 4 servings (6 c.) zucchini noodles with lemon vinaigrette

Directions:

1. Season the shrimp with salt and pepper.
2. In a medium saucepan over medium heat, heat the oil. Add the shallot and garlic and cook until the shallot softens and the garlic is fragrant, for about 3 minutes. Add the shrimp, cover, and cook until opaque, 2–3 minutes on each side. Using a slotted spoon, transfer the shrimp to a large plate.
3. Add the wine, lemon juice, and sriracha to the saucepan, and stir to combine. Bring the mixture to a boil, then reduce the heat and simmer until the liquid is reduced by about half, 3 minutes. Add the butter and stir until melted, about 3 minutes. Return the shrimp to the saucepan and toss to coat. Add the parsley and stir to combine.
4. Into each of 4 containers, place 1 1/2 c of zucchini noodles with lemon vinaigrette, and top with 3/4 c of scampi.

Nutrition:

Calories 364

Total fat 21 g.

Saturated fat 6 g.

Protein 37 g.

Total carbs 10 g.

Fiber 2 g.

Sugar 6 g.

Sodium 557 mg.

Maple-Mustard Salmon

Preparation time: 10 minutes, plus 30 minutes marinating time

Cooking time: 20 minutes

Servings: 4

Ingredients:

- Nonstick cooking spray
- 1/2 c. 100 % maple syrup
- 2 tbsps Dijon mustard

- 1/4 tsp. salt
- 4 (5-oz.) salmon fillets
- 4 servings (4 c.) roasted broccoli with shallots
- 4 servings (2 c.) parleyed whole-wheat couscous

Directions:

1. Preheat the oven to 400 °F. Line a baking sheet with aluminum foil and coat with cooking spray.
2. In a medium bowl, whisk together the maple syrup, mustard, and salt until smooth.
3. Put the salmon fillets into the bowl and toss to coat. Cover and place in the refrigerator to marinate for at least 30 minutes and up to overnight.
4. Shake off excess marinade from the salmon fillets and place them on the prepared baking sheet, leaving a 1-in. space between each fillet. Discard the extra marinade.
5. Bake for about 20 minutes until the salmon is opaque and a thermometer inserted in the thickest part of a fillet reads 145 °F.

6. Into each of 4 resealable containers, place 1 salmon fillet, 1 c of roasted broccoli with shallots, and 1/2 c of parleyed whole-wheat couscous.

Nutrition:

Calories 601

Total fat 29 g.

Saturated fat 4 g.

Protein 36 g.

Total carbs 51 g.

Fiber 3 g.

Sugar 23 g.

Sodium 610 mg.

Chicken Salad with Grapes and Pecans

Preparation time: 15 minutes
Cooking time: 5 minutes
Servings: 4

Ingredients:

- 1/3 c. unsalted pecans, chopped
- 10 oz. cooked skinless, boneless chicken breast or rotisserie chicken, finely chopped
- 1/2 medium yellow onion, finely chopped
- 1 celery stalk, finely chopped
- 3/4 c. red or green seedless grapes, halved
- 1/4 c. light mayonnaise
- 1/4 c. nonfat plain Greek yogurt
- 1 tbsp. Dijon mustard
- 1 tbsp. dried parsley
- 1/4 tsp. salt
- 1/8 tsp. freshly ground black pepper
- 1 c. shredded romaine lettuce
- 4 (8-in.) whole-wheat pitas

Directions:

1. Heat a small skillet over medium-low heat to toast the pecans. Cook the pecans until fragrant, about 3 minutes. Remove from the heat and set aside to cool.

2. In a medium bowl, mix the chicken, onion, celery, pecans, and grapes.
3. In a small bowl, whisk together the mayonnaise, yogurt, mustard, parsley, salt, and pepper. Spoon the sauce over the chicken mixture and stir until well combined.
4. Into each of 4 containers, place 1/4 c of lettuce and top with 1 c of chicken salad. Store the pitas separately until ready to serve.
5. When ready to eat, stuff the serving of salad and lettuce into 1 pita.

Nutrition:

Calories 418

Total fat 14 g.

Saturated fat 2 g.

Protein 31 g.

Total carbs 43 g.

Fiber 6 g.

Roasted Vegetables

Preparation time: 14 minutes

Cooking time: 17 minutes

Servings: 3

Ingredients:

- 4 tbsp. olive oil, reserve some for greasing
- 2 heads, large garlic, tops sliced off
- 2 large eggplants/aubergines, tops removed, cubed
- 2 large shallots, peeled, quartered
- 1 large carrot, peeled, cubed
- 1 large parsnip, peeled, cubed
- 1/2 tsp. rosemary leaves
- 1 small green bell pepper, deseeded, ribbed, cubed
- 1 small red bell pepper, deseeded, ribbed, cubed
- 1/2 lb. Brussels sprouts, halved, do not remove cores
- 1 sprig, large thyme, leaves picked Sea salt, coarse-grained

For garnish

- 1 large lemon, halved, 1/2 squeezed, 1/2 sliced into smaller wedges
- 1/8 c. fennel bulb, minced

Directions:

1. From 425 °F or 220°C preheat the oven for at least 5 minutes before using.
2. Line deep roasting pan with aluminum foil; lightly grease with oil. Tumble in bell peppers, Brussels sprouts, carrots, eggplants, garlic, parsnips, rosemary leaves, shallots, and thyme. Add a pinch of sea salt; drizzle in remaining oil and lemon juice. Toss well to combine.
3. Cover roasting pan with a sheet of aluminum foil. Place this on the middle rack of the oven. Bake for 20–30 minutes. Remove aluminum foil. Roast, for another 5–10 minutes, or until the

vegetables are brown at the edges. Remove roasting pan from oven. Cool slightly before ladling equal portions into plates.

4. Garnish with fennel and a wedge of lemon. Squeeze lemon juice on top of the dish before eating.

Nutrition:

Calories 163

Total fat 4.2 g.

Saturated fat 0.8 g.

Cholesterol 0 mg.

Sodium 861 mg.

Total carbs 22.5 g.

Fiber 6.3 g.

Sugar 2.3 g.

Protein 9.2 g.

Millet Pilaf

Preparation time: 10 minutes

Cooking time: 15 minutes

Servings: 4

Ingredients:

- 1 c. millet
- 2 tomatoes, rinsed, seeded, and chopped
- 1 3/4 cups filtered water
- 2 tbsps extra-virgin olive oil
- 1/4 c. chopped dried apricot
- Zest of 1 lemon
- Juice of 1 lemon
- 1/2 c. fresh parsley, rinsed and chopped
- Himalayan pink salt
- Freshly ground black pepper

Directions:

1. In an electric pressure cooker, combine the millet, tomatoes, and water. Lock the lid into place, select Manual and High Pressure, and cook for 7 minutes.
2. When the beep sounds, quick release the pressure by pressing Cancel and twisting the steam valve to the Venting position. Carefully remove the lid.
3. Stir in olive oil, apricot, lemon zest, lemon juice, and parsley. Taste, season with salt and pepper and serve.

Nutrition:

Calories 270

Total fat 8 g.

Total carbohydrates 42 g.

Fiber 5 g.

Sugar 3 g.

Protein 6 g.

Sweet and Sour Onions

Preparation time: 10 minutes

Cooking time: 11 minutes

Servings: 4

Ingredients:

- 4 large onions, halved
- 2 garlic cloves, crushed
- 3 c. vegetable stock
- 1 1/2 tbsp. balsamic vinegar
- 1/2 teaspoon Dijon mustard
- 1 tbsp. sugar

Directions:

1. Combine onions and garlic in a pan. Fry for 3 minutes, or till softened.
2. Pour stock, vinegar, Dijon mustard, and sugar. Bring to a boil.
3. Reduce heat. Cover and let the mixture simmer for 10 minutes.

4. Remove from the heat. Continue stirring until the liquid is reduced and the onions are brown. Serve.

Nutrition:

Calories 203

Total Fat 41.2 g.

Saturated Fat 0.8 g.

Cholesterol 0 mg.

Sodium 861 mg.

Total Carbohydrates 29.5 g.

Fiber 16.3 g.

Sugar 29.3 g.

Protein 19.2 g.

Sautéed Apples and Onions

Preparation time: 14 minutes

Cooking time: 16 minutes

Servings: 3

Ingredients:

- 2 c. dry cider
- 1 large onion, halved
- 2 c. vegetable stock
- 4 apples, sliced into wedges
- Pinch of salt
- Pinch of pepper

Directions:

1. Combine cider and onion in a saucepan. Bring to a boil until the onions are cooked and the liquid is almost gone.
2. Pour the stock and the apples. Season with salt and pepper. Stir occasionally. Cook for about 10 minutes or until the apples are tender but not mushy. Serve.

Nutrition:

Calories 343

Total Fat 51.2 g.

Saturated Fat 0.8 g.

Cholesterol 0 mg.

Sodium 861 mg.

Total Carbohydrates 22.5 g.

Fiber 6.3 g.

Sugar 2.3 g.

Protein 9.2 g.

Zucchini Noodles with Portobello Mushrooms

Preparation time: 14 minutes

Cooking time: 16 minutes

Servings: 3

Ingredients:

- 1 zucchini, processed into spaghetti-like noodles
- 3 garlic cloves, minced
- 2 white onions, thinly sliced
- 1 thumb-sized ginger, julienned
- 1 lb. chicken thighs
- 1 lb. portobello mushrooms, sliced into thick slivers
- 2 c. chicken stock

- 3 c. water
- Pinch of sea salt, add more if needed
- Pinch of black pepper, add more if needed
- 2 tsp. sesame oil
- 4 tbsp. coconut oil, divided
- 1/4 c. fresh chives, minced, for garnish

Directions:

1. Pour 2 tbsps of coconut oil into a large saucepan. Fry mushroom slivers in batches for 5 minutes or until seared brown. Set aside. Transfer these to a plate.
2. Sauté the onion, garlic, and ginger for 3 minutes or until tender. Add in chicken thighs, cooked mushrooms, chicken stock, water, salt, and pepper, and stir well. Bring to a boil.
3. Decrease gradually the heat and allow simmering for 20 minutes or until the chicken is forking tender. Add sesame oil.
4. Serve by placing an equal amount of zucchini noodles into bowls. Ladle soup and garnish with chives.

Nutrition:

Calories 163

Total fat 4.2 g.

Saturated fat 0.8 g.

Cholesterol 0 mg.

Sodium 861 mg.

Total carbs 22.5 g.

Fiber 6.3 g.

Sugar 2.3 g.

Protein 9.2 g.

Dinner

Cauliflower Mac and Cheese

Preparation time: 5 minutes

Cooking time: 25 minutes

Servings: 4

Ingredients:

- 1 cauliflower head, torn into florets
- Salt and black pepper, as needed
- 1/4 c. almond milk, unsweetened
- 1/4 c. heavy cream
- 3 tbsp. butter, preferably grass-fed
- 1 c. cheddar cheese, shredded

Directions:

1. Preheat the oven to 450 °F.
2. Melt the butter in a small microwave-safe bowl and heat it for 30 seconds.

3. Pour the melted butter over the cauliflower florets along with salt and pepper. Toss them well.
4. Place the cauliflower florets in a parchment paper-covered large baking sheet.
5. Bake them for 15 minutes or until the cauliflower is crisp-tender.
6. Once baked, mix the heavy cream, cheddar cheese, almond milk, and the remaining butter in a large microwave-safe bowl and heat it on high heat for 2 minutes or until the cheese mixture is smooth. Repeat the procedure until the cheese has melted.
7. Finally, stir in the cauliflower to the sauce mixture and coat well.

Nutrition:

Calories 294 Fat 23 g.
Carbohydrates 7 g.
Proteins 11 g.

Easy Egg Salad

Preparation time: 5 minutes

Cooking time: 15–20 minutes

Servings: 4

Ingredients:

- 6 eggs, preferably free-range
- 1/4 tsp. salt
- 2 tbsp. mayonnaise
- 1 tsp. lemon juice
- 1 tsp. Dijon mustard
- Pepper, to taste
- Lettuce leaves, to serve

Directions:

1. Keep the eggs in a saucepan of water and pour cold water until it covers the egg by another 1 in.
2. Bring to a boil and then remove the eggs from heat.
3. Peel the eggs under cold running water.

4. Transfer the cooked eggs into a food processor and pulse them until chopped.
5. Stir in the mayonnaise, lemon juice, salt, Dijon mustard, pepper and mix them well.
6. Taste for seasoning and add more if required.
7. Serve in the lettuce leaves.

Nutrition:

Calories 166

Fat 14 g.

Carbohydrates - 0.85 g.

Proteins 10 g.

Sodium 132 mg.

Baked Chicken Legs

Preparation time: 10 minutes

Cooking time: 40 minutes

Servings: 6

Ingredients:

- 6 chicken legs
- 1/4 tsp. black pepper
- 1/4 c. butter
- 1/2 tsp. sea salt
- 1/2 tsp. smoked paprika
- 1/2 tsp. garlic powder

Directions:

1. Preheat the oven to 425 °F.
2. Pat the chicken legs with a paper towel to absorb any excess moisture.
3. Marinate the chicken pieces by first applying the butter over them and then with the seasoning. Set it aside for a few minutes.

4. Bake them for 25 minutes. Turnover and bake for further 10 minutes or until the internal temperature reaches 165 °F.
5. Serve them hot.

Nutrition:

Calories 236

Fat 16 g.

Carbohydrates 0 g.

Protein 22 g.

Sodium 314 mg.

Creamed Spinach

Preparation time: 5 minutes
Cooking time: 10 minutes
Servings: 4
Ingredients:

- 3 tbsp. butter
- 1/4 tsp. black pepper
- 4 cloves of garlic, minced
- 1/4 tsp. sea salt
- 10 oz. baby spinach, chopped
- 1 tsp. Italian seasoning
- 1/2 c. heavy cream
- 3 oz. cream cheese

Directions:

1. Melt butter in a large sauté pan over medium heat.
2. Once the butter has melted, spoon in the garlic and sauté for 30 seconds or until aromatic.
3. Spoon in the spinach and cook for 3–4 minutes or until wilted.
4. Add all the remaining ingredients to it and continuously stir until the cream cheese melts and the mixture gets thickened.
5. Serve hot.

Nutrition:

Calories 274

Fat 27 g.

Carbohydrates 4 g.

Protein 4 g.

Sodium 114 mg.

Stuffed Mushrooms

Preparation time: 10 minutes

Cooking time: 20 minutes

Servings: 4

Ingredients:

- 4 portobello mushrooms, large
- 1/2 c. mozzarella cheese, shredded
- 1/2 c. marinara, low-sugar
- Olive oil spray

Directions:

1. Preheat the oven to 375 °F.

2. Take out the dark gills from the mushrooms with the help of a spoon.
3. Keep the mushroom stem upside down and spoon it with 2 tbsps of marinara sauce and mozzarella cheese.
4. Bake for 18 minutes or until the cheese is bubbly.

Nutrition:

Calories 113 Fat 6 g.

Carbohydrates 4 g.

Protein 7 g.

Sodium 14 mg.

Vegetable Soup

Preparation time: 10 minutes
Cooking time: 30 minutes
Servings: 5

Ingredients:

- 8 c. vegetable broth
- 2 tbsp. olive oil
- 1 tbsp. Italian seasoning1 onion, large and diced
- 2 bay leaves, dried
- 2 bell pepper, large and diced
- Sea salt and black pepper, as needed
- 4 cloves of garlic, minced
- 28 oz. tomatoes, diced
- 1 cauliflower head, medium and torn into florets
- 2 c. green beans, trimmed and chopped

Directions:

1. Heat oil in a Dutch oven over medium heat.
2. Once the oil becomes hot, stir in the onions and pepper.
3. Cook for 10 minutes or until the onion is softened and browned.
4. Spoon in the garlic and sauté for a minute or until fragrant.

5. Add all the remaining ingredients to it. Mix until everything comes together.
6. Bring the mixture to a boil. Lower the heat and cook for further 20 minutes or until the vegetables have softened.

Nutrition:

Calories 79 Fat 2 g.

Carbohydrates 8 g.

Protein 2 g.

Sodium 187 mg.

Pork Chop Diane

Preparation time: 10 minutes

Cooking time: 20 minutes

Servings: 4

Ingredients:

- 1/4 c. low-sodium chicken broth
- 1 tbsp. freshly squeezed lemon juice
- 2 tsps. Worcestershire sauce
- 2 tsps. Dijon mustard

- 4 (5-oz.) boneless pork top loin chops
- 1 tsp. extra-virgin olive oil
- 1 tsp. lemon zest
- 1 tsp. butter
- 2 tsps. chopped fresh chives

Directions:

1. Blend together the chicken broth, lemon juice, Worcestershire sauce, and Dijon mustard and set it aside.
2. Season the pork chops lightly.
3. Situate a large skillet over medium-high heat and add the olive oil.
4. Cook the pork chops, turning once, until they are no longer pink, about 8 minutes per side.
5. Put aside the chops.
6. Pour the broth mixture into the skillet and cook until warmed through and thickened, about 2 minutes.
7. Blend lemon zest, butter, and chives.
8. Garnish with a generous spoonful of sauce.

Nutrition:

Calories 200

Fat 8 g.

Carbohydrates 1 g.

Autumn Pork Chops with Red Cabbage and Apples

Preparation time: 15 minutes
Cooking time: 30 minutes
Servings: 4
Ingredients:

- 1/4 c. apple cider vinegar
- 2 tbsps granulated sweetener
- 4 (4-oz.) pork chops, about 1 in. thick
- 1 tbsp. extra-virgin olive oil
- 1/2 red cabbage, finely shredded
- 1 sweet onion, thinly sliced
- 1 apple, peeled, cored, and sliced
- 1 tsp. chopped fresh thyme

- Salt and pepper, to taste

Directions:

1. Mix vinegar and sweetener. Set it aside.
2. Season the pork with salt and pepper.
3. Position a big skillet over medium-high heat and add the olive oil.
4. Cook the pork chops until no longer pink, turning once, about 8 minutes per side.
5. Put chops aside.
6. Add the cabbage and onion to the skillet and sauté until the vegetables have softened, for about 5 minutes.
7. Add the vinegar mixture and the apple slices to the skillet and bring the mixture to a boil.
8. Adjust heat to low and simmer, covered, for 5 additional minutes.
9. Return the pork chops to the skillet, along with any accumulated juices and thyme, cover, and cook for 5 more minutes.

Nutrition:

Calories 223

Carbohydrates 12 g.

Fiber 3 g.

Chipotle Chili Pork Chops

Preparation time: 4 hours
Cooking time: 20 minutes
Servings: 4
Ingredients:

- Juice and zest of 1 lime
- 1 tbsp. extra-virgin olive oil
- 1 tbsp. chipotle chili powder
- 2 tsps. minced garlic
- 1 tsp. ground cinnamon
- Pinch sea salt
- 4 (5-oz.) pork chops Lime wedges

Directions:

1. Combine the lime juice and zest, oil, chipotle chili powder, garlic, cinnamon, and salt in a resealable plastic bag. Add the pork chops. Remove as much air as possible and seal the bag.
2. Marinate the chops in the refrigerator for at least 4 hours, and up to 24 hours, turning them several times.
3. Ready the oven to 400 °F and set a rack on a baking sheet. Let the chops rest at room temperature for 15 minutes, then arrange them on the rack and discard the remaining marinade.
4. Roast the chops until cooked through, turning once, about 10 minutes per side.
5. Serve with lime wedges.

Nutrition:

Calories 204

Carbohydrates 1 g.

Sugar 1 g.

Orange-Marinated Pork Tenderloin

Preparation time: 2 hours

Cooking time: 30 minutes

Servings: 4

Ingredients:

- 1/4 c. freshly squeezed orange juice
- 2 tsps. orange zest
- 2 tsps. minced garlic
- 1 tsp. low-sodium soy sauce
- 1 tsp. grated fresh ginger
- 1 tsp. honey
- 1 1/2 lbs. pork tenderloin roast
- 1 tbsp. extra-virgin olive oil

Directions:

1. Blend together the orange juice, zest, garlic, soy sauce, ginger, and honey.
2. Pour the marinade into a resealable plastic bag and add the pork tenderloin.

3. Remove as much air as possible and seal the bag. Marinate the pork in the refrigerator, turning the bag a few times, for 2 hours.
4. Preheat the oven to 400 °F.
5. Pull out tenderloin from the marinade and discard the marinade.
6. Position big ovenproof skillet over medium-high heat and add the oil.
7. Sear the pork tenderloin on all sides, about 5 minutes in total.
8. Position skillet to the oven and roast for 25 minutes.
9. Put aside for 10 minutes before serving.

Nutrition:

Calories 228

Carbohydrates 4 g.

Sugar 3 g.

Homestyle Herb Meatballs

Preparation time: 10 minutes

Cooking time: 15 minutes

Servings: 4

Ingredients:

- 1/2-lb. lean ground pork
- 1/2-lb. lean ground beef
- 1 sweet onion, finely chopped
- 1/4 c. bread crumbs
- 2 tbsps chopped fresh basil
- 2 tsps. minced garlic
- 1 egg
- Salt and pepper, to taste

Directions:

1. Preheat the oven to 350 °F.
2. Prepare a baking tray with parchment paper and set it aside.
3. In a large bowl, mix together the pork, beef, onion, bread crumbs, basil, garlic, egg, salt, and pepper until very well mixed.

4. Roll the meat mixture into 2-in. meatballs.
5. Transfer the meatballs to the baking sheet and bake until they are browned and cooked through, about 15 minutes.
6. Serve the meatballs with your favorite marinara sauce and some steamed green beans.

Nutrition:

Calories 332

Carbohydrates 13 g.

Sugar 3 g

Lime-Parsley Lamb Cutlets

Preparation time: 4 hours

Cooking time: 10 minutes

Servings: 4

Ingredients:

- 1/4 c. extra-virgin olive oil
- 1/4 c. freshly squeezed lime juice

- 2 tbsps lime zest
- 2 tbsps chopped fresh parsley
- 12 lamb cutlets (about 1 1/2 lbs. total)
- Salt and pepper, to taste

Directions:

1. Scourge the oil, lime juice, zest, parsley, salt, and pepper.
2. Pour the marinade into a resealable plastic bag.
3. Add the cutlets to the bag and remove as much air as possible before sealing.
4. Marinate the lamb in the refrigerator for about 4 hours, turning the bag several times.
5. Preheat the oven to broil.
6. Remove the chops from the bag and arrange them on an aluminum foil-lined baking sheet. Discard the marinade.
7. Broil the chops for 4 minutes per side for medium doneness.
8. Let the chops rest for 5 minutes before serving.

Nutrition:

Calories 413

Carbohydrates 1 g.

Protein 31 g.

Mediterranean Steak Sandwiches

Preparation time: 1 hour

Cooking time: 10 minutes

Servings: 4

Ingredients:

- 2 tbsps extra-virgin olive oil
- 2 tbsps balsamic vinegar
- 2 tsps. garlic
- 2 tsps. lemon juice
- 2 tsps. fresh oregano
- 1 tsp. fresh parsley
- 1-pound flank steak
- 4 whole-wheat pitas
- 2 c. shredded lettuce

- 1 red onion, thinly sliced
- 1 tomato, chopped
- 1 oz. low-sodium feta cheese

Directions:

1. Scourge olive oil, balsamic vinegar, garlic, lemon juice, oregano, and parsley.
2. Add the steak to the bowl, turning to coat it completely.
3. Marinate the steak for 1 hour in the refrigerator, turning it over several times.
4. Preheat the broiler. Line a baking sheet with aluminum foil.
5. Put the steak out of the bowl and discard the marinade.
6. Situate the steak on the baking sheet and broil for 5 minutes per side for medium.
7. Set aside for 10 minutes before slicing.
8. Stuff the pitas with the sliced steak, lettuce, onion,

tomato, and feta.

Nutrition:

Calories 344

Carbohydrates 22 g.

Fiber 3 g

Roasted Beef with Peppercorn Sauce

Preparation time: 10 minutes

Cooking time: 90 minutes

Servings: 4

Ingredients:

- 1 1/2 lbs. top rump beef roast
- 3 tsps. extra-virgin olive oil
- 3 shallots, minced
- 2 tsps. minced garlic
- 1 tbsp. green peppercorns
- 2 tbsps dry sherry
- 2 tbsps all-purpose flour

- 1 c. sodium-free beef broth
- Salt and pepper, to taste

Directions:

1. Heat the oven to 300 °F.
2. Season the roast with salt and pepper.
3. Position a big skillet over medium-high heat and add 2 tsps of olive oil.
4. Brown the beef on all sides, about 10 minutes in total, and transfer the roast to a baking dish.
5. Roast until desired doneness, about 1 1/2 hours for medium. When the roast has been in the oven for 1 hour, start the sauce.
6. In a medium saucepan over medium-high heat, sauté the shallots in the remaining 1 tsp of olive oil until translucent, about 4 minutes.
7. Stir in the garlic and peppercorns, and cook for another minute. Whisk in the sherry to deglaze the pan.
8. Whisk in the flour to form a thick paste, cooking for 1 minute and stirring constantly.

9. Fill in the beef broth and whisk for 4 minutes. Season the sauce.

10. Serve the beef with a generous spoonful of sauce.

Nutrition:

Calories 330

Carbohydrates 4 g.

Protein 36 g.

Coffee-and-Herb-Marinated Steak

Preparation time: 2 hours
Cooking time: 10 minutes
Servings: 3
Ingredients:

- 1/4 c. whole coffee beans
- 2 tsps. garlic
- 2 tsps. rosemary
- 2 tsps. thyme
- 1 tsp. black pepper

- 2 tbsps apple cider vinegar
- 2 tbsps extra-virgin olive oil
- 1-pound flank steak, trimmed of visible fat

Directions:

1. Place the coffee beans, garlic, rosemary, thyme, and black pepper in a coffee grinder or food processor and pulse until coarsely ground.
2. Transfer the coffee mixture to a resealable plastic bag and add the vinegar and oil. Shake to combine.
3. Add the flank steak and squeeze the excess air out of the bag. Seal it. Marinate the steak in the refrigerator for at least 2 hours, occasionally turning the bag over.
4. Preheat the broiler. Line a baking sheet with aluminum foil.
5. Pull the steak out and discard the marinade.
6. Position steak on the baking sheet and broil until it is done to your liking.
7. Put aside for 10 minutes before cutting it.
8. Serve with your favorite side dish.

Nutrition:

Calories 313

Fat 20 g.

Protein 31 g.

Traditional Beef Stroganoff

Preparation time: 10 minutes

Cooking time: 30 minutes

Servings: 4

Ingredients:

- 1 tsp. extra-virgin olive oil
- 1-lb. top sirloin, cut into thin strips
- 1 c. sliced button mushrooms
- 1/2 sweet onion, finely chopped
- 1 tsp. minced garlic
- 1 tbsp. whole-wheat flour
- 1/2 c. low-sodium beef broth
- 1/4 c. dry sherry
- 1/2 c. fat-free sour cream

- 1 tbsp. chopped fresh parsley
- Salt and pepper, to taste

Directions:

1. Position the skillet over medium-high heat and add the oil.
2. Sauté the beef until browned, about 10 minutes, then remove the beef with a slotted spoon to a plate and set it aside.
3. Add the mushrooms, onion, and garlic to the skillet and sauté until lightly browned, for about 5 minutes.
4. Whisk in the flour and then whisk in the beef broth and sherry.
5. Return the sirloin to the skillet and bring the mixture to a boil.
6. Reduce the heat to low and simmer until the beef is tender, about 10 minutes.
7. Stir in the sour cream and parsley. Season with salt and pepper.

Nutrition:

Calories 257

Carbohydrates 6 g.

Fiber 1 g.

Chicken and Roasted Vegetable Wraps

Preparation time: 10 minutes

Cooking time: 20 minutes

Servings: 4

Ingredients:

- 1/2 small eggplant
- 1 red bell pepper
- 1 medium zucchini
- 1/2 small red onion, sliced
- 1 tbsp. extra-virgin olive oil
- 2 (8-oz.) cooked chicken breasts, sliced
- 4 whole-wheat tortilla wraps
- Salt and pepper, to taste

Directions:

1. Preheat the oven to 400 °F.
2. Wrap a baking sheet with foil and set it aside.
3. In a large bowl, toss the eggplant, bell pepper, zucchini, and red onion with olive oil.
4. Transfer the vegetables to the baking sheet and lightly season with salt and pepper.
5. Roast the vegetables until soft and slightly charred, about 20 minutes.
6. Divide the vegetables and chicken into four portions.
7. Wrap 1 tortilla around each portion of chicken and grilled vegetables, and serve.

Nutrition:

Calories 483

Carbohydrates 45 g.

Fiber 3 g.

Spicy Chicken Cacciatore

Preparation time: 20 minutes

Cooking time: 1 hour

Servings: 6

Ingredients:

- 1 (2-lb.) chicken
- 1/4 c. all-purpose flour
- 2 tbsps extra-virgin olive oil
- 3 slices bacon
- 1 sweet onion
- 2 tsps. minced garlic
- 4 oz. button mushrooms, halved
- 1 (28-oz.) can of low-sodium stewed tomatoes
- 1/2 c. red wine
- 2 tsps. chopped fresh oregano
- 2 tsps. red pepper flakes
- Salt and pepper, to taste

Directions:

1. Cut the chicken into pieces 2 drumsticks, 2 thighs, 2 wings, and 4 breast pieces.
2. Dredge the chicken pieces in the flour and season each piece with salt and pepper.
3. Place a large skillet over medium-high heat and add the olive oil.
4. Brown the chicken pieces on all sides, about 20 minutes in total. Transfer the chicken to a plate.
5. Cook the chopped bacon in the skillet for 5 minutes. With a slotted spoon, transfer the cooked bacon to the same plate as the chicken.
6. Pour off most of the oil from the skillet, leaving just a light coating. Sauté the onion, garlic, and mushrooms in the skillet until tender, about 4 minutes.
7. Stir in the tomatoes, wine, oregano, and red pepper flakes.

8. Bring the sauce to a boil. Return the chicken and bacon, plus any accumulated juices from the plate, to the skillet.

9. Reduce the heat to low and simmer until the chicken is tender, about 30 minutes.

Nutrition:

Calories 230

Carbohydrates 14 g.

Fiber 2 g.

Scallion Sandwich

Preparation time: 10 minutes

Cooking time: 10 minutes

Servings: 1

Ingredients:

- 2 slices wheat bread
- 2 tsps. butter, low-fat
- 2 scallions, sliced thinly
- 1 tbsp of parmesan cheese, grated
- 3/4 c of cheddar cheese, reduced fat, grated

Directions:

1. Preheat the Air fryer to 356 °F.
2. Spread butter on a slice of bread. Place inside the cooking basket with the butter side facing down.
3. Place cheese and scallions on top. Spread the rest of the butter on the other slice of bread Put it on top of the sandwich and sprinkle it with parmesan cheese.
4. Cook for 10 minutes.

Nutrition:

Calorie 154

Carbohydrate 9 g.

Fat 2.5 g.

Protein 8.6 g.

Fiber 2.4 g.

Lean Lamb and Turkey Meatballs with Yogurt

Preparation time: 10 minutes

Servings: 4

Cooking time: 8 minutes

Ingredients:

For the Meatballs

- 1 egg white
- 4 oz. ground lean turkey
- 1 lb of ground lean lamb
- 1 tsp. each of cayenne pepper, ground coriander, red chili pastes, salt, and ground cumin
- 2 garlic cloves, minced
- 1 1/2 tbsps parsley, chopped
- 1 tbsp. mint, chopped
- 1/4 c of olive oil

For the Yogurt

- 2 tbsps of buttermilk
- 1 garlic clove, minced

- 1/4 c. mint, chopped
- 1/2 c of Greek yogurt, non-fat
- Salt to taste

Directions:

1. Set the air fryer to 390 °F.
2. Mix all the ingredients for the meatballs in a bowl. Roll and mold them into golf-size round pieces. Arrange in the cooking basket. Cook for 8 minutes.
3. While waiting, combine all the ingredients for the mint yogurt in a bowl. Mix well.
4. Serve the meatballs with mint yogurt. Top with olives and fresh mint.

Nutrition:

Calorie 154

Carbohydrate 9 g.

Fat 2.5 g.

Protein 8.6 g.

Fiber 2.4 g.

Air Fried Section and Tomato

Preparation time: 10 minutes

Cooking time: 5 minutes

Servings: 2

Ingredients:

- 1 aubergine, sliced thickly into 4 disks
- 1 tomato, sliced into 2 thick disks
- 2 tsp. feta cheese, reduced-fat
- 2 fresh basil leaves, minced
- 2 balls, small buffalo mozzarella, reduced-fat, roughly torn
- Pinch of salt
- Pinch of black pepper

Directions:

1. Preheat air fryer to 330 °F.
2. Spray a small amount of oil into the air fryer basket. Fry the aubergine slices for 5 minutes or

until golden brown on both sides. Transfer to a plate.

3. Fry tomato slices in batches for 5 minutes or until seared on both sides.
4. To serve, stack salad starting with an aborigine base, buffalo mozzarella, basil leaves, tomato slice, and 1/2-teaspoon feta cheese.
5. Top of with another slice of aborigine and 1/2 tsp. feta cheese. Serve.

Nutrition:

Calorie 140.3

Carbohydrate 26.6

Fat 3.4 g.

Protein 4.2 g.

Fiber 7.3 g.

Cheesy Salmon Fillets

Preparation time: 15 minutes

Cooking time: 20 minutes

Servings: 2–3

Ingredients:

For the Salmon Fillets

- 2 pieces, 4 oz. each salmon fillets, choose even cuts
- 1/2 c. sour cream, reduced-fat
- 1/4 c. cottage cheese, reduced-fat
- 1/4 c. Parmigiano-Reggiano cheese, freshly grated

For the Garnish

- Spanish paprika
- 1/2-piece lemon, cut into wedges

Directions:

1. Preheat the air fryer to 330 °F.
2. To make the salmon fillets, mix sour cream, cottage cheese, and Parmigiano-Reggiano cheese in a bowl.
3. Layer salmon fillets in the Air fryer basket. Fry for 20 minutes or until cheese turns golden brown.
4. To assemble, place a salmon fillet and sprinkle paprika. Garnish with lemon wedges and squeeze lemon juice on top.
Serve.

Nutrition:

Calorie 274

Carbohydrate 1 g.

Fat 19 g.

Protein 24 g.

Fiber 0.5 g.

Salmon with Asparagus

Preparation time: 5 minutes

Cooking time: 10 minutes

Servings: 3

Ingredients:

- 1 lb. salmon, sliced into fillets
- 1 tbsp. olive oil
- Salt and pepper, as needed
- 2 cloves of garlic, minced
- Zest and juice of 1/2 lemon
- 1 tbsp. butter, salted

Directions:

1. Spoon in the butter and olive oil into a large pan and heat it over medium-high heat.
2. Once it becomes hot, place the salmon and season it with salt and pepper.

3. Cook for 4 minutes per side and then cook the other side.
4. Stir in the garlic and lemon zest to it.
5. Cook for further 2 minutes or until slightly browned.
6. Off the heat and squeeze the lemon juice over it.
7. Serve it hot.

Nutrition:

Calories 409

Carbohydrates 2.7 g.

Proteins 32.8 g.

Fat 28.8 g.

Sodium 497 mg.

Shrimp in Garlic Butter

Preparation time: 5 minutes

Cooking time: 20 minutes

Servings: 4

Ingredients:

- 1 lb. shrimp, peeled and deveined
- 1/4 tsp. red pepper flakes
- 6 tbsp. butter, divided
- 1/2 c. chicken stock
- Salt and pepper, as needed
- 2 tbsp. parsley, minced
- 5 cloves of garlic, minced
- 2 tbsp. lemon juice

Directions:

1. Heat a large, bottomed skillet over medium-high heat.
2. Spoon in 2 tbsps of the butter and melt it. Add the shrimp.

3. Season it with salt and pepper. Sear for 4 minutes or until shrimp gets cooked.
4. Transfer the shrimp to a plate and stir in the garlic.
5. Sauté for 30 seconds or until aromatic.
6. Pour the chicken stock and whisk it well. Allow it to simmer for 5– 10 minutes or until it has reduced to half.
7. Spoon the remaining butter, red pepper, and lemon juice into the sauce. Mix.
8. Continue cooking for another 2 minutes.
9. Take off the pan from the heat and add the cooked shrimp to it.
10. Garnish with parsley and transfer to the serving bowl.

Nutrition:

Calories 307

Carbohydrates 3 g.

Proteins 27 g.

Fat 20 g.

Sodium 522 mg.

Cobb Salad

Preparation time: 5 minutes
Cooking time: 5 minutes
Servings: 1
Ingredients:

- 4 cherry tomatoes, chopped
- 1/4 c. bacon, cooked and crumbled
- 1/2 of 1 avocado, chopped
- 2 oz. chicken breast, shredded
- 1 egg, hardboiled
- 2 c. mixed green salad
- 1 oz. feta cheese, crumbled

Directions:

1. Toss all the ingredients for the cobb salad in a large mixing bowl and toss well.
2. Serve and enjoy it.

Nutrition:

Calories 307

Carbohydrates 3 g.

Proteins 27 g.

Fat 20 g.

Sodium 522 mg.

Salad

Thai Quinoa Salad

Preparation time: 10 minutes

Cooking time: 0 minutes

Servings: 1–2

Ingredients:

For the Dressing

- 1 tbsp. sesame seed
- 1 tsp. chopped garlic
- 1 tsp. lemon, fresh juice
- 3 tsp. apple cider vinegar
- 2 tsp. tamari, gluten-free.
- 1/4 c of tahini (sesame butter)
- 1 pitted date
- 1/2 tsp. salt
- 1/2 tsp. toasted sesame oil

For the Salad

- 1 c of quinoa, steamed
- 1 big handful of arugulas
- 1 tomato cut into pieces
- 1/4 of the red onion, diced

Directions:

1. Add filtered water and all the ingredients for the dressing into a small blender. Mix.
2. Steam the quinoa in a steamer or a rice pan, then set aside.
3. Combine the quinoa, the arugula, the tomatoes sliced, the red onion diced on a serving plate or bowl, add the Thai dressing and serve with a spoon.

Nutrition:

Calories 100

Carbohydrates 12 g.

Green Goddess Bowl and Avocado Cumin Dressing

Preparation time: 10 minutes

Cooking time: 0 minutes

Servings: 1–2

Ingredients:

For the Avocado Cumin Dressing

- 1 avocado
- 1 tbsp. cumin powder
- 2 limes, freshly squeezed
- 1 c of filtered water
- 1/4 seconds. sea salt
- 1 tbsp. olive extra-virgin olive oil
- Cayenne pepper dash
- Optional: 1/4 tsp. smoked pepper

For the Lemon Tahini Dressing

- 1/4 c of tahini (sesame butter)
- 1/2 c of filtered water (more if you want it thinner; less if you want it thicker)

- 1/2 lemon, freshly squeezed
- 1 clove of minced garlic
- 3/4 tsp. sea salt (Celtic Gray, Himalayan, Redmond Real Salt)
- 1 tbsp. olive extra-virgin olive oil
- Black pepper taste

For the Salad

- 3 c of kale, chopped
- 1/2 c of broccoli flowers, chopped
- 1/2 zucchini (make spiral noodles)
- 1/2 c of kelp noodles, soaked and drained
- 1/3 c of cherry tomatoes, halved
- 2 tsp. hemp seeds

Directions:

1. Gently steam the kale and the broccoli (set the steam for 4 minutes), set aside.
2. Mix the zucchini noodles and kelp noodles and toss with a generous portion of the smoked avocado

cumin dressing. Add the cherry tomatoes and stir again.

3. Place the steamed kale and broccoli and drizzle with the lemon tahini dressing. Top the kale and the broccoli with the noodles and tomatoes and sprinkle the whole dish with the hemp seeds.

Nutrition:

Calories 89

Carbohydrates 11 g.

Fat 1.2 g.

Protein 4 g.

Sweet and Savory Salad

Preparation time: 10 minutes

Cooking time: 0 minutes

Servings: 1–2

Ingredients:

- 1 big head of butter lettuce
- 1/2 of cucumber, sliced
- 1 pomegranate, seed, or 1/3 c of seed

- 1 avocado, 1 cubed
- 1/4 c of shelled pistachio, chopped

For the Dressing

- 1/4 c of apple cider vinegar
- 1/2 c of olive oil
- 1 clove of garlic, minced

Directions:

1. Put the butter lettuce in a salad bowl.
2. Add the remaining ingredients and toss with the salad dressing.

Nutrition:

Calories 68

Carbohydrates 8 g.

Fat 1.2 g.

Protein 2 g.

Kale Pesto's Pasta

Preparation time: 10 minutes

Cooking time: 0 minutes

Servings: 1–2

Ingredients:

- 1 bunch of kale
- 2 c of fresh basil
- 1/4 c of extra-virgin olive oil
- 1/2 c of walnuts
- 2 limes, freshly squeezed
- Sea salt and chili pepper
- 1 zucchini, noodle (spiralizer)
- Optional: garnish with chopped asparagus, spinach leaves, and tomato.

Directions:

1. The night before, soak the walnuts in order to improve absorption.

2. Put all the kale pesto ingredients in a blender and blend until the consistency of the cream is reached.
3. Add the zucchini noodles and enjoy.

Nutrition:

Calories 55

Carbohydrates 9 g

Fat 1.2 g.

Beet Salad with Basil Dressing

Preparation time: 10 minutes
Cooking time: 0 minutes
Servings: 4
Ingredients:
For the Dressing

- 1/4 c. blackberries
- 1/4 c. extra-virgin olive oil
- Juice of 1 lemon

- 2 tbsps minced fresh basil
- 1 tsp. poppy seeds
- A pinch of sea salt

For the Salad

- 2 celery stalks, chopped
- 4 cooked beets, peeled and chopped
- 1 c. blackberries
- 4 c. spring mix

Directions:

1. To make the dressing, mash the blackberries in a bowl. Whisk in the oil, lemon juice, basil, poppy seeds, and sea salt.
2. To make the salad: Add the celery, beets, blackberries, and spring mix to the bowl with the dressing.
3. Combine and serve.

Nutrition:

Calories 192

Fat 15 g.

Carbohydrates 15 g.

Protein 2 g.

Basic Salad with Olive Oil Dressing

Preparation time: 10 minutes

Cooking time: 0 minute

Servings: 4

Ingredients:

- 1 c. coarsely chopped iceberg lettuce
- 1 c. coarsely chopped romaine lettuce
- 1 c. fresh baby spinach
- 1 large tomato, hulled and coarsely chopped
- 1 c. diced cucumber
- 2 tbsps extra-virgin olive oil
- 1/4 tsp of sea salt

Directions:

1. In a bowl, combine the spinach and lettuces. Add the tomato and cucumber.
2. Drizzle with oil and sprinkle with sea salt.
3. Mix and serve.

Nutrition:

Calories 77

Fat 4 g.

Carbohydrates 3 g.

Protein 1 g.

Spinach and Orange Salad with Oil Drizzle

Preparation time: 10 minutes

Cooking time: 0 minute

Servings: 4

Ingredients:

- 4 c. fresh baby spinach
- 1 blood orange, coarsely chopped
- 1/2 red onion, thinly sliced
- 1/2 shallot, finely chopped
- 2 tbsp. minced fennel fronds
- Juice of 1 lemon
- 1 tbsp. extra-virgin olive oil
- Pinch sea salt

Directions:

1. In a bowl, toss together the spinach, orange, red onion, shallot, and fennel fronds.
2. Add the lemon juice, oil, and sea salt.
3. Mix and serve.

Nutrition:

Calories 79

Fat 2 g.

Carbohydrates 8 g.

Protein 1 g.

Fruit Salad with Coconut-Lime Dressing

Preparation time: 5 minutes

Cooking time: 0 minutes

Servings: 4

Ingredients:

For the Dressing

- 1/4 c. full-fat canned coconut milk
- 1 tbsp. raw honey
- Juice of 1/2 lime
- Pinch sea salt
- For the salad
- 2 bananas, thinly sliced

- 2 mandarin oranges, segmented
- 1/2 c. strawberries, thinly sliced
- 1/2 c. raspberries
- 1/2 c. blueberries

Directions:

1. To make the dressing: Whisk all the dressing ingredients in a bowl.
2. To make the salad: Add the salad ingredients to a bowl and mix.
3. Drizzle with the dressing and serve.

Nutrition:

Calories 141

Fat 3 g.

Carbohydrates 30 g.

Protein 2 g.

Cranberry and Brussels Sprouts with Dressing

Preparation time: 10 minutes

Cooking time: 0 minute

Servings: 4

Ingredients:

For the Dressing

- 1/3 c. extra-virgin olive oil
- 2 tbsp. apple cider vinegar
- 1 tbsp. pure maple syrup
- Juice of 1 orange
- 1/2 tbsp. dried rosemary
- 1 tbsp. scallion, whites only
- Pinch sea salt

For the Salad

- 1 bunch scallions, greens only, finely chopped
- 1 c. Brussels sprouts, stemmed, halved, and thinly sliced

- 1/2 c. fresh cranberries
- 4 c. fresh baby spinach

Directions:

1. To make the dressing: In a bowl, whisk the dressing ingredients.
2. To make the salad: Add the scallions, Brussels sprouts, cranberries, and spinach to the bowl with the dressing.
3. Combine and serve.

Nutrition:

Calories 267

Fat 18 g.

Carbohydrates 26 g.

Protein 2 g.

Parsnip, Carrot, and Kale Salad with Dressing

Preparation time: 10 minutes

Cooking time: 0 minutes

Servings: 4

Ingredients:

For the Dressing

- 1/3 c. extra-virgin olive oil
- Juice of 1 lime
- 2 tbsp. minced fresh mint leaves
- 1 tsp. pure maple syrup
- Pinch sea salt

For the Salad

- 1 bunch kale, chopped
- 1/2 parsnip, grated
- 1/2 carrot, grated
- 2 tbsp. sesame seeds

Directions:

1. To make the dressing, mix all the dressing ingredients in a bowl.
2. To make the salad, add the kale to the dressing and massage the dressing into the kale for 1 minute.
3. Add the parsnip, carrot, and sesame seeds.
4. Combine and serve.

Nutrition:

Calories 214

Fat 2 g.

Carbohydrates 12 g.

Protein 2 g.

Tomato Toasts

Preparation time: 5 minutes
Cooking time: 5 minutes
Servings: 4
Ingredients:

- 4 slices of sprouted bread toasts
- 2 tomatoes, sliced
- 1 avocado, mashed
- 1 tsp. olive oil
- 1 pinch of salt
- 3/4 teaspoon ground black pepper

Directions:

1. Blend together the olive oil, mashed avocado, salt, and ground black pepper.
2. When the mixture is homogenous, spread it over the sprouted bread.
3. Then place the sliced tomatoes over the toasts.

Nutrition:

Calories 125

Fat 11.1 g.

Carbohydrates 7.0 g.

Protein 1.5 g.

Every Day Salad

Preparation time: 10 minutes

Cooking time: 40 minutes

Servings: 6

Ingredients:

- 5 halved mushrooms
- 6 halved cherry (plum) tomatoes
- 6 rinsed lettuce leaves
- 10 olives
- 1/2 chopped cucumber
- Juice from 1/2 key lime
- 1 tsp. olive oil
- Pure sea salt

Directions:

1. Tear rinsed lettuce leaves into medium pieces and put them in a medium salad bowl.

2. Add mushrooms halves, chopped cucumber, olives, and cherry tomato halves into the bowl. Mix well. Pour olive and key lime juice over the salad.
3. Add pure sea salt to taste. Mix it all till it is well combined.

Nutrition:

Calories 88

Carbohydrates 11 g.

Fat: .5 g.

Protein: .8 g.

Super-Seedy Salad with Tahini Dressing

Preparation time: 10 minutes

Cooking time: 0 minutes

Servings: 1–2

Ingredients:

- 1 slice stale sourdough, torn into chunks
- 50 g. mixed seeds
- 1 tsp. cumin seeds
- 1 tsp. coriander seeds
- 50 g. baby kale
- 75 g. long-stemmed broccoli, blanched for a few minutes then roughly chopped
- 1/2 red onion, thinly sliced
- 100 g. cherry tomatoes, halved
- 1/2 a small bunch-flat-leaf parsley, torn

For the Dressing

- 100 ml. natural yogurt
- 1 tbsp. tahini
- 1 lemon, juiced

Directions:

1. Heat the oven to 200 °C/fan 180 °C/gas 6. Put the bread into a food processor and pulse into very rough breadcrumbs. Put into a bowl with the mixed seeds and spices, season, and spray well with oil. Tip

onto a non-stick baking tray and roast for 15–20 minutes, stirring and tossing regularly, until golden brown.

2. Whisk together the dressing ingredients, some seasoning, and a splash of water in a large bowl. Tip the baby kale, broccoli, red onion, cherry tomatoes, and flat-leaf parsley into the dressing, and mix well. Divide between 2 plates and top with the crispy breadcrumbs and seeds.

Nutrition:

Calories 78

Carbohydrates 6 g Fat 2 g.

Protein 1.5 g.

Vegetable Salad

Preparation time: 10 minutes

Cooking time: 0 minutes

Servings: 1–2

Ingredients:

- 4 c. each of raw spinach and romaine lettuce
- 2 c. each of cherry tomatoes, sliced cucumber, chopped baby carrots, chopped red, orange, and yellow bell pepper
- 1 c. each of chopped broccoli, sliced yellow squash, zucchini, and cauliflower.

Directions:

1. Wash all these vegetables.
2. Mix in a large mixing bowl and top off with a non-fat or low-fat dressing of your choice.
3. **Nutrition:**

   Calories 48

   Carbohydrates 11 g.

   Protein 3 g.

Greek Salad

Preparation time: 10 minutes

Cooking time: 0 minutes

Servings: 1–2

Ingredients:

- 1 Romaine head, torn in bits
- 1 cucumber sliced
- 1-pint cherry tomatoes, halved
- 1 green pepper, thinly sliced
- 1 onion sliced into rings
- 1 c. kalamata olives
- 1 1/2 c. feta cheese, crumbled

For dressing combine:

- 1 c. olive oil
- 1/4 c. lemon juice
- 2 tsp. oregano
- Salt and pepper

Directions:

1. Put the ingredients on a plate.
2. Drizzle the dressing over the salad.

Nutrition:

Calories 107

Carbohydrates 18 g.

Fat 1.2 g

Protein 1 g.

Alkaline Spring Salad

Preparation time: 10 minutes

Cooking time: 0 minutes

Servings: 1–2

Ingredients:

- 4 c. seasonal approved greens of your choice
- 1 c. cherry tomatoes
- 1/4 c. walnuts
- 1/4 c. approved herbs of your choice

For the Dressing

- 3–4 key limes
- 1 tbsp of homemade raw sesame "tahini" butter Sea
- salt and cayenne pepper

Directions:

1. First, get the juice of the key limes. In a small bowl, whisk together the key lime juice with the homemade raw sesame "tahini" butter. Add sea salt and cayenne pepper, to taste.
2. Cut the cherry tomatoes in half.
3. In a large bowl, combine the greens, cherry tomatoes, walnuts, and herbs. Pour the dressing on top and "massage" with your hands.
4. Let the greens soak up the dressing. Add more sea salt, cayenne pepper, and herbs on top if you wish.

Nutrition:

Calories 77

Carbohydrates 11 g.

Fresh Tuna Salad

Preparation time: 10 minutes
Cooking time: none
Servings: 3

Ingredients:

- 1 can tuna (6 oz.)
- 1/3 c. fresh cucumber, chopped
- 1/3 c. fresh tomato, chopped
- 1/3 c. avocado, chopped
- 1/3 c. celery, chopped
- 2 garlic cloves, minced
- 4 tsp. olive oil
- 2 tbsp. lime juice
- Pinch of black pepper

Directions:

1. Prepare the dressing by combining olive oil, lime juice, minced garlic, and black pepper.
2. Mix the remaining ingredients in a salad bowl and drizzle with the dressing.

Nutrition:

Carbohydrates 4.8 g.

Protein 14.3 g.

Total sugars 1.1 g.

Calories 212 g.

Roasted Portobello Salad

Preparation time: 10 minutes

Cooking time: none

Servings: 4

Ingredients:

- 1 1/2 lb. portobello mushrooms, stems trimmed
- 3 heads Belgian endive, sliced
- 1 small red onion, sliced
- 4 oz. blue cheese
- 8 oz. mixed salad greens

For the Dressing

- 3 tbsp. red wine vinegar
- 1 tbsp. Dijon mustard

- 2/3 c. olive oil
- Salt and pepper to taste

Directions:

1. Preheat the oven to 450 °F.
2. Prepare the dressing by whisking together vinegar, mustard, salt, and pepper. Slowly add olive oil while whisking.
3. Cut the mushrooms and arrange them on a baking sheet, stem-side up. Coat the mushrooms with some dressing and bake for 15 minutes.
4. In a salad bowl toss the salad greens with onion, endive, and cheese. Sprinkle with the dressing.
5. Add mushrooms to the salad bowl.

Nutrition:

Calories 501

Carbohydrates 22.3 g.

Protein 14.9 g.

Total sugars 2.1 g.

Shredded Chicken Salad

Preparation time: 5 minutes

Cooking time: 10 minutes

Servings: 6

Ingredients:

- 2 chicken breasts, boneless, skinless
- 1 head iceberg lettuce, cut into strips
- 2 bell peppers, cut into strips
- 1 fresh cucumber, quartered, sliced
- 3 scallions, sliced
- 2 tbsp. chopped peanuts
- 1 tbsp. peanut vinaigrette
- Salt to taste
- 1 c of water

Directions:

1. In a skillet simmer one cup of salted water.
2. Add the chicken breasts, cover, and cook on low for 5 minutes. Remove the cover. Then remove the chicken from the skillet and shred with a fork.
3. In a salad bowl mix the vegetables with the cooled chicken, season with salt and sprinkle with peanut vinaigrette and chopped peanuts.

Nutrition:

Carbohydrates 9 g.

Protein 11.6 g.

Total sugars 4.2 g.

Calories 117

Broccoli Salad

Preparation time: 10 minutes

Cooking time: none

Servings: 6

Ingredients:

- 1 medium head broccoli, raw, florets only
- 1/2 c. red onion, chopped
- 12 oz. turkey bacon, chopped, fried until crisp
- 1/2 c. cherry tomatoes, halved
- 1/4 c. sunflower kernels
- 3/4 c. raisins
- 3/4 c. mayonnaise
- 2 tbsp. white vinegar

Directions:

1. In a salad bowl combine the broccoli, tomatoes, and onion.
2. Mix mayo with vinegar and sprinkle over the broccoli.
3. Add the sunflower kernels, raisins, and bacon and toss well.

Nutrition:

Calories 220

Carbohydrates 17.3 g.

Protein 11 g.

Total sugars 10 g.

Cherry Tomato Salad

Preparation time: 10 minutes

Cooking time: none

Servings: 6

Ingredients:

- 40 cherry tomatoes, halved
- 1 c. mozzarella balls, halved
- 1 c. green olives, sliced
- 1 can (6 oz.) black olives, sliced
- 2 green onions, chopped
- 3 oz. roasted pine nuts

For the Dressing

- 1/2 c. olive oil

- 2 tbsp. red wine vinegar
- 1 tsp. dried oregano
- Salt and pepper to taste

Directions:

1. In a salad bowl, combine the tomatoes, olives, and onions.
2. Prepare the dressing by combining olive oil with red wine vinegar, dried oregano, salt, and pepper.
3. Sprinkle with the dressing and add the nuts.
4. Let marinate in the fridge for 1 hour.

Nutrition:

Carbohydrates 10.7 g.

Protein 2.4 g.

Total sugars 3.6 g.

Ground Turkey Salad

Preparation time: 10 minutes

Cooking time: 35 minutes

Servings: 6

Ingredients:

- 1 lb. lean ground turkey
- 1/2-in. ginger, minced
- 2 garlic cloves, minced
- 1 onion, chopped
- 1 tbsp. olive oil
- 1 bag lettuce leaves (for serving)
- 1/4 c. fresh cilantro, chopped
- 2 tsp. coriander powder
- 1 tsp. red chili powder
- 1 tsp. turmeric powder
- Salt to taste
- 4 c. water

For the Dressing:

- 2 tbsp. fat-free yogurt
- 1 tbsp. sour cream, non-fat
- 1 tbsp. low-fat mayonnaise
- 1 lemon, juiced
- 1 tsp. red chili flakes
- Salt and pepper to taste

Directions:

1. In a skillet, sauté the garlic and ginger in olive oil for 1 minute. Add onion and season with salt. Cook for 10 minutes over medium heat.
2. Add the ground turkey and sauté for 3 more minutes. Add the spices (turmeric, red chili powder, and coriander powder).
3. Add 4 c of water and cook for 30 minutes, covered.
4. Prepare the dressing by combining yogurt, sour cream, mayo, lemon juice, chili flakes, salt, and pepper.

5. To serve arrange the salad leaves on serving plates and place the cooked ground turkey on them. Top with the dressing.

Nutrition:

Carbohydrates 9.1 g.

Protein 17.8 g.

Total sugars 2.5 g.

Calories 176

Asian Cucumber Salad

Preparation time: 10 minutes

Cooking time: none

Servings: 6

Ingredients:

- 1 lb. cucumbers, sliced
- 2 scallions, sliced
- 2 tbsp. sliced pickled ginger, chopped

- 1/4 c. cilantro
- 1/2 red jalapeño, chopped
- 3 tbsp. rice wine vinegar
- 1 tbsp. sesame oil
- 1 tbsp. sesame seeds

Directions:

1. In a salad bowl combine all ingredients and toss them together.

Nutrition:

Carbohydrates 5.7 g.

Protein 1 g.

Total sugars 3.1 g.

Calories 52

Cauliflower Tofu Salad

Preparation time: 10 minutes

Cooking time: 15 minutes

Servings: 4

Ingredients:

- 2 c. cauliflower florets, blended
- 1 fresh cucumber, diced
- 1/2 c. green olives, diced
- 1/3 c. red onion, diced
- 2 tbsp. toasted pine nuts
- 2 tbsp. raisins
- 1/3 c. feta, crumbled
- 1/2 c. pomegranate seeds
- 2 lemons (juiced, zest grated)
- 8 oz. tofu
- 2 tsp. oregano

- 2 garlic cloves, minced
- 1/2 tsp. red chili flakes
- 3 tbsp. olive oil
- Salt and pepper to taste

Directions:

1. Season the blended cauliflower with salt and transfer to a strainer to drain.
2. Prepare the marinade for the tofu by combining 2 tbsp. lemon juice, 1.5 tbsp. olive oil, minced garlic, chili flakes, oregano, salt, and pepper. Coat the tofu in the marinade and set it aside.
3. Preheat the oven to 450 °F.
4. Bake the tofu on a baking sheet for 12 minutes.
5. In a salad bowl mix the remaining marinade with onions, cucumber, cauliflower, olives, and raisins. Add in the remaining olive oil and grated lemon zest.
6. Top with tofu, pine nuts, feta, and pomegranate seeds.

Nutrition:

Carbohydrates 34.1 g.

Protein 11.1 g.

Total sugars 11.5 g.

Calories 328

Scallop Caesar Salad

Preparation time: 5 minutes

Cooking time: 2 minutes

Servings: 2

Ingredients:

- 8 sea scallops
- 4 c. romaine lettuce
- 2 tsp. olive oil
- 3 tbsp. Caesar salad dressing
- 1 tsp. lemon juice
- Salt and pepper to taste

Directions:

1. In a frying pan heat olive oil and cook the scallops in one layer no longer than 2 minutes on both sides. Season with salt and pepper to taste.
2. Arrange the lettuce on plates and place scallops on top.

3. Pour over the Caesar dressing and lemon juice.

Nutrition:

Carbohydrates 14 g.

Protein 30.7 g.

Total sugars 2.2 g.

Calories 340 g.

www.ingramcontent.com/pod-product-compliance
Lightning Source LLC
LaVergne TN
LVHW020424070526
838199LV00003B/263